DAY TRADING VOL 4

The top 4 strategies professionals use to make a living day trading at the market open

Follow the "Million-Dollar Margin Club MMCVisions" to get new release updates on their Amazon Author's Page
https://amzn.to/3UOplQJ

Million-Dollar-Margin Club YouTube channel:
bit.ly/3tNzDFA

Million-Dollar-Margin Club's #1 Best Sellers

DAY TRADING VOL 4 DAY TRADING THE OPEN
Author: The Million-Dollar Margin Club MMCVision
Printed Version ISBN: 979-8-9890300-9-5
Publisher: MMCVisions Publishing
Publication Date: August 2024
For permission requests, contact: MMCVisions@gmail.com
Website: million-dollar-marginclub.com
YouTube Channel Million-Dollar-Margin Club

Disclaimer: The information provided in this trading guide, should not be construed as financial or investment advice. You should conduct your own research and consult with a licensed financial advisor before making any investment decisions based on the content of this book. Do not live trade using the guidelines in this book until you have followed the advice of a licensed professional. By reading this book the reader agrees to hold the author harmless and not responsible for any losses incurred directly or indirectly from any and all the information contained in this book including, but not limited to, any strategies, errors, omissions, tools, layouts, studies, indicators or inaccuracies contained within.

Other Books by MMCVisions Publishing
Available on Amazon

Welcome to DAY TRADING

A Complete Beginner's Guide and Workbook for Day Trading Using the RV Strategy

- Complete guidelines on how to trade the RV Strategy
- Details on how to open your first account with helpful suggestions of brokerages within the U.S. and offshore
- Learn studies and indicators
- The Million-dollar Margin Club's daily stock rating system
- Learn the importance of stock scanners
- 10 candlestick patterns rated for accuracy
- Learn range-bound channel trading and identifying support and resistance levels
- How stock consolidation can bring profits
- Create a day trading plan with a new way to manage risk
- 10 Things to remember when range-bound trading
- Advanced guidelines to understanding your own trade analysis
- Details on executing trades with chart examples from professional traders
- Importance of controlling your emotions while day trading
- Learn details on how to trade with Fibonacci Retracements, VWAP, SMA, EMA, RSI, Volume Profile, ADX, Level II, Time and Sales, and ATR
- Worksheets and logs with examples provided

10 Candlestick Patterns and The Ratings you Must Know Before you Trade

82% Accurate

When Identified, Bear flags will continue a trend an average of 82% of the time.

DAY TRADING VOL 1: Make a Living Day Trading Million-Dollar Margin Club

DAY TRADING VOL 1

Finally a Complete Step by Step Guide on How to Day Trade and Scalp Using a Range Bound Strategy

Make a Living Day Trading

The Million-Dollar Margin Club's Beginners' RV Strategy

What is the RV Strategy

The RV Strategy is a new way of range-bound scalping within channels that are defined in a specific way.

- Within these channels, traders rely on multiply aligned support and resistance levels, Fibonacci Retracement levels, and many indicators typically used by day traders to implement their trades. The range of the trades are dependent on ATR (Average True Range) levels of a particular stock calculated from the previous close of day.

- The stocks traded are large caps that are consolidating but this strategy can work well with any stock size. The ideal time of trading usually starts at 30 minutes after the market opens. The per trade risk is solely based on share size within the identified channels' price range. A simple formula is applied to find your share size to help increase your profit and mitigate any losses.

- Experience in scalping is helpful but not necessary to trade the RV Strategy as it is specifically designed for beginners and advanced traders alike. The rating system and work sheets included in chapter 14 will help you find the right stocks to trade each day.

As you continue to read you will see the entire strategy laid out with examples on charts, details of the indicators commonly used for the **RV Strategy** along with very helpful general day trading information. Helpful worksheets to implement this strategy complete this volume.

Other Books by MMCVisions Publishing
Available on Amazon

What's Inside

- Unique Candlestick Pattern Rating System
- The Important Candlestick Patterns You Should Know
- Understand Candlestick Patterns for any Trading Style
- Quizzes and Games to Help Learn Candlestick Patterns
- Flashcards to Help Remember Candlestick Patterns

*"Mastering candlestick patterns is
the key to profitable trading"*
- John Bull Bear

THE CANDLESTICK PATTERN PLAYBOOK

DAY TRADING VOL 2

DAY TRADING VOL 2
A Professional Trader's Guide to Success

THE CANDLESTICK PATTERN PLAYBOOK

**Memorize Candlestick Patterns with
Charts • Puzzles • Games • Flashcards**

DAY TRADING your way to Fast Profits

TABLE OF CONTENTS

Have fun as You Learn Your Candlestick Patterns with These Helpful Flashcards

Other Books by MMCVisions Publishing
Available on Amazon

"Candlestick Mastery Beginner to Pro in 66 Patterns" is an engaging guide that hones your technical analysis skills through a series of hands-on exercises. With challenges ranging from recognizing named candlestick patterns to predicting their direction, this book offers a dynamic learning experience, culminating in the ultimate test of naming the patterns.

Challenges Include:

• Beginner: Find the Named Candlestick Patterns
• Advanced: Find and Name the Candlestick Patterns
• Expert: Name and Predict the Direction of the Candlestick Pattern
• Professional: Name the Candlestick Patterns

Course and Study Guide for
"The Candlestick Pattern Playbook"

Candlestick Mastery Beginner to Pro in 66 Patterns

DAY TRADING VOL 3

Learn Technical Analysis with
Charts and Challenges

Candlestick Mastery
Beginner to Pro
in 66 Patterns

17th century Munehisa Homma contemplates his next trade

This image provided by John Bull Bear historical archives was created shortly after the disastrous abacus accident that cost Munehisa his ring finger. Some believe the accident caused the mathematical error that triggered the catastrophic rice shortage of 1687 which resulted in many citizens losing their life savings.

DAY TRADING VOL 3

Candlestick Patterns

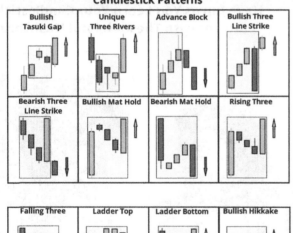

Bullish Tasuki Gap | Unique Three Rivers | Advance Block | Bullish Three Line Strike

Bearish Three Line Strike | Bullish Mat Hold | Bearish Mat Hold | Rising Three

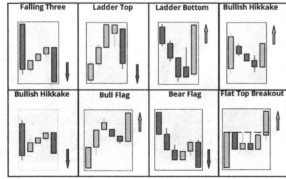

Falling Three | Ladder Top | Ladder Bottom | Bullish Hikkake

Bullish Hikkake | Bull Flag | Bear Flag | Flat Top Breakout

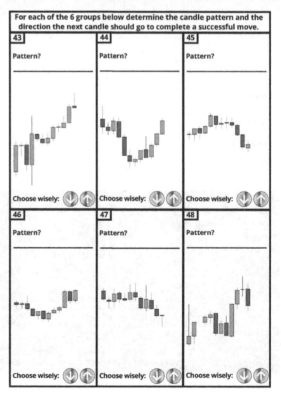

For each of the 6 groups below determine the candle pattern and the direction the next candle should go to complete a successful move.

43 Pattern?

44 Pattern?

45 Pattern?

Choose wisely:

46 Pattern?

47 Pattern?

48 Pattern?

Choose wisely:

Other Books by MMCVisions Publishing
Available on Amazon

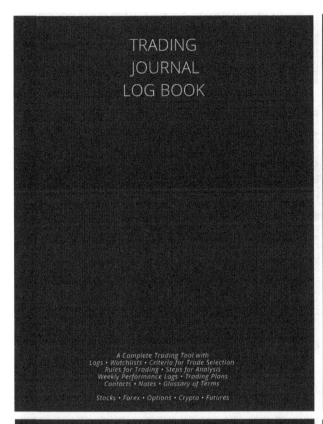

TRADING
JOURNAL
LOG BOOK

A Complete Trading Tool with
Logs • Watchlists • Criteria for Trade Selection
Rules for Trading • Steps for Analysis
Weekly Performance Logs • Trading Plans
Contacts • Notes • Glossary of Terms

Stocks • Forex • Options • Crypto • Futures

COMPANION BOOK TO
DAY TRADING VOL 1

Additional Tools and Worksheets for
Day Trading Using a Range Bound Strategy

Stock Rating System and Log
Sheets for the RV Strategy

Million-Dollar Margin Club's Beginner Strategy

OPTIONS TRADING
LOGBOOK AND JOURNAL

TRADE LIKE A PROFESSIONAL

THE MILLION-DOLLAR MARGIN CLUB SHARES
4 TRADERS' PROFITABLE STRATEGIES USED IN
WORLDWIDE COMPETITION

FUTURES TRADING
LOGBOOK AND JOURNAL

TRADE LIKE A PROFESSIONAL

THE MILLION-DOLLAR MARGIN CLUB SHARES
4 TRADERS' PROFITABLE STRATEGIES USED IN
WORLDWIDE COMPETITION

Other Books by MMCVisions Publishing
Available on Amazon

CRYPTO TRADING LOGBOOK AND JOURNAL

TRADE LIKE A PROFESSIONAL

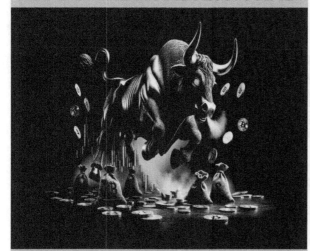

THE MILLION-DOLLAR MARGIN CLUB SHARES 4 TRADERS' PROFITABLE STRATEGIES USED IN WORLDWIDE COMPETITION

STOCK TRADING LOGBOOK AND JOURNAL

TRADE LIKE A PROFESSIONAL

THE MILLION-DOLLAR MARGIN CLUB SHARES 4 TRADERS' PROFITABLE STRATEGIES USED IN WORLDWIDE COMPETITION

PENNY STOCK TRADING LOGBOOK AND JOURNAL

TRADE LIKE A PROFESSIONAL

THE MILLION-DOLLAR MARGIN CLUB SHARES 4 TRADERS' PROFITABLE STRATEGIES USED IN WORLDWIDE COMPETITION

FOREX TRADING LOGBOOK AND JOURNAL

TRADE LIKE A PROFESSIONAL

THE MILLION-DOLLAR MARGIN CLUB SHARES 4 TRADERS' PROFITABLE STRATEGIES USED IN WORLDWIDE COMPETITION

Special Thanks to the Million-Dollar Margin Club's
Book Review and Editing Team's newest members

The Million-Dollar Margin Club is committed to releasing high quality, entertaining, and educational books. The MMC welcomes creative ideas and reviews from the trading community for their pre-published and even, already published books.
Team memebers' names can be immortalized
in the pages of MMC publications.

If you would like to join the exclusive Million-Dollar-Margin Club
and participate in this unique opportunity,
please email:
mmcvisions@gmail.com
with the subject line **Join the MMC**

Get Ready to Trade the Open

TABLE OF CONTENTS

Day Trading the Open

Welcome to Volume 4 of the esteemed series crafted by The Million-Dollar Margin Club, a distinguished collective of professional traders dedicated to elevating the craft of trading.

History was made with the first 3 volumes

DAY TRADING VOL 1
How to Make a Living Day Trading

introduced the revolutionary RV Strategy, a range-bound technique trading large cap stocks that has resonated deeply within the trading community, becoming a cornerstone strategy for many.

DAY TRADING VOL 2:
The Candlestick Pattern Playbook

expanded the trader's toolkit by identifying candlestick patterns, complete with a unique rating system to help traders prioritize which patterns to master based on their trading style and market conditions.

DAY TRADING VOL 3:
Candlestick Mastery Beginner to Pro in 66 Patterns

took a creative turn, making the learning process both enjoyable and practical. It served as a visual and interactive guide to identifying critical candlestick patterns, offering traders a method to enhance their pattern recognition skills through engaging, chart-based puzzles and examples.

Now Introducing Vol 4

Day Trading the Open

Day Trading the Open dives into the exhilarating world of intraday trading, scalping during the market open. This volume is tailored for those who have grasped the essentials of day trading and are ready to tackle the market at its most volatile. The first 90 minutes after the market opens are both dynamic and unpredictable, presenting a unique set of challenges and opportunites that only the most adept traders can navigate successfully.

In this book, we discuss four scalping strategies based on different time-bound charts that are designed for the market open, all developed with the precision and depth that traders have come to expect from The Million-Dollar Margin Club. Each strategy focuses on precise price level entries working within a paramenter that utilizes a trader's already developed scalping skills to capitalize on fast profits. For those ready to engage with this volume, remember that scalping the open is not merely about quick profits; its about disciplined execution, rapid decision making, and meticulous risk management. This book aims to cultivate these qualities among its readers, encouraging you to make the most of every trading day's crucial opening moments.

We thank you for your trust in The Million-Dollar Margin Club as we continue to serve the trading community with dedication and insight. May this volume inspire you, challenge you, and above all, equip you to achieve greater success in your trading endeavors.

CHAPTER 1

RECAP DAY TRADING VOLS 1-3
TEST YOUR MEMORY SKILLS

Refresh your basic skills with
DAY TRADING VOL 1

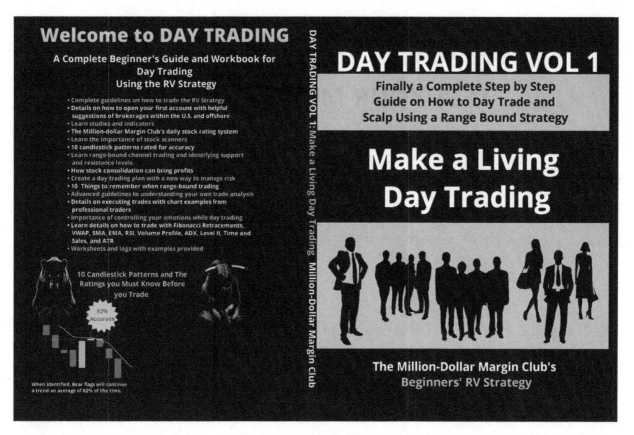

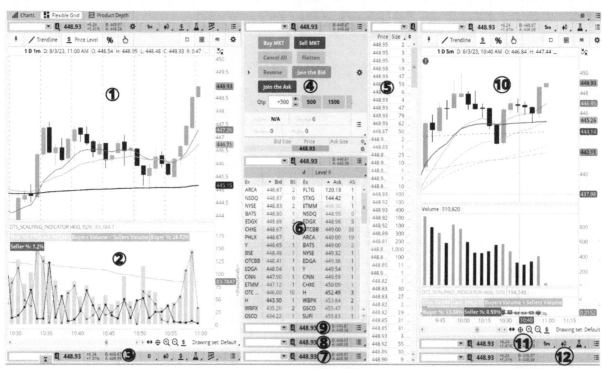

Understanding the Two Trading Styles

Scalping: Involves buying and selling securities within a very short time frame, often minutes or even seconds, with the goal of capturing small price movements. Scalpers thrive on the high liquidity and fast order execution available during the market open, capitalizing on identified profit targets. They make dozens of trades an hour, with the goal of accumulating small profits that can add up to substantial returns by the end of the day.

Day Trading: Day trading is similar to scalping in that all positions are closed daily, before the market closes. However, day traders typically hold their positions for a longer duration than scalpers, from several minutes to several hours. Day trading involves a deeper analysis of the markets, more than just intraday trends and often does not require the rapid-fire execution that scalping does.

Understanding Long vs Short Trading Styles

Going long: When traders go long, they buy securities with the expectation that the price will rise. Long positions are often associated with bullish market sentiments. In scalping, going long means quickly entering and exiting positions to take advantage of small upward price movements. Essentially buying at a lower price then selling at a higher price.

Shorting: Short selling, or shorting, involves selling borrowed securities, with the intention of buying them back later at a lower price. This strategy is used when a trader anticipates a drop in price levels. In the context of scalping, shorting is a critical technique, especially during market corrections or when bearish trends dominate the early trading session. Most scalpers will ride a stock's price direction both up and down to capitalize on profits in both directions.

Scalping Techniques for the Market Open

While the specific strategies for scalping will be detailed later, here are some broad techniques that are essential for successful scalping during the market open:

Rapid Order Execution

Scalpers must be able to enter and exit trades quickly. This requires a trading platform that supports high speed order execution and real-time data processing.

Leverage and Margin

Understanding and managing leverage is crucial since scalping often involves the use of significant leverage to maximize the returns on small price movements. Working with the right broker that offers a 4 to 1 margin is very helpful.

Strategy Preparation

Setting up your charts with the right indicators, support, resistance and profit taking levels, as well as following your chosen strategy, are essential for trading the open.

Risk Management

Even though profits and losses per trade are minimal, the cumulative effect can be significant. Effective risk management techniques, following your strategy and setting mental stop-loss orders, having a maximum loss per trade and overall daily loss limit laid out in a detailed trading plan is vital. Remember, win or lose, every trade and day are successful if you follow your trading plan.

Most professional traders will tell new traders looking to make money quickly, that scalping is the fastest way to become profitable. However, scalping the market open is not suitable for everyone. It demands intense focus, quick decision making, and an in-depth understanding of short term market mechanics. Those who master it can be highly rewarded.

The following chapters will introduce four specific scalping strategies most effectively utilized within the first 90 minutes of the opening; each tailored to different market conditions and personal trading styles to ensure traders can make the most out of the first critical minutes of the trading day.

Market Orders, Limit Orders, and Trading Fees Explained

When buying shares of stock on a stock exchange, there are two primary types of orders you can use: market orders and limit orders. These orders dictate how your trade is executed and at what price. Here's an explanation of the key differences between the two:

1. Market Order is an instruction to buy or sell a stock immediately at the best available current market price. The execution of a market order is typically fast because it's designed to be executed promptly, regardless of the specific price. When you place a market order, you're essentially telling the brokerage to execute the trade as quickly as possible, even if it means paying a slightly different price than the last quoted price.

Advantages:

High probability of execution. Market orders are usually executed quickly, especially for highly liquid stocks.

Disadvantages:

Lack of price control. You might end up buying the stock at a higher price than expected if the market moves rapidly between the time you place the order and the time it's executed. In fast moving volatilite markets, the execution price of a market order might differ significantly from the last quoted price.

2. Limit Order buys or sells a stock at a specific price or better. When you place a limit order, you specify the maximum price you're willing to pay (for a buy order) or the minimum price you're willing to accept (for a sell order). The trade will only be executed at or better than the specified price.

Advantages:

Price control. You can dictate the price at which you're willing to buy or sell. Protection against unexpected price changes: Limit orders protect you from unfavorable price movements, as the trade will only be executed at or better than your specified price.

Disadvantages:

No guarantee of execution. If the stock doesn't have a sufficient quantity of shares or reach your specified price, the limit order may only fill a portion of your share size or not be executed at all.

Trading Fees and Payment for Order Flow:

Some brokers charge fees for executing market orders. These fees contribute to the cost of executing the trade and maintaining the trading infrastructure. Additionally, some brokers have relationships with market makers or high frequency trading firms that pay them for directing their customer orders to those firms for execution. This practice is called "payment for order flow."

With payment for order flow, the broker receives compensation from the market maker for sending customer orders to them. This compensation is typically derived from the difference between the Bid (buying) and Ask (selling) price, known as the "spread." While this allows brokers to offer commission-free trades, it has raised questions about potential conflicts of interest and whether the practice might result in less favorable execution prices for customers.

Direct access and trading fees:

Some brokers offer direct market access which allows traders to interact directly with the exchange's order book. This can lead to faster execution speeds and potentially better control over the execution price. However, brokers that provide direct access may charge trading fees to cover the cost of the advanced technology and infrastructure required to facilitate these trades.

A market order is executed immediately at the best available current market price according to the national best bid offer price (NBBO) which fills your trade at or better than the current market price, while a limit order is executed only at a specified price or better. Market orders prioritize speed of execution over price, while limit orders prioritize price, but might not guarantee immediate execution. It's important to consider the current market conditions and your trading objectives when deciding which type of order to use. Some brokers charge trading fees for executing trades and may also participate in payment for order flow arrangements, where they receive compensation from market makers for routing customer orders. Others may provide commision-free trading by relying on payment for order flow to generate revenue. It's essential for traders to consider these factors when choosing a broker and selecting their preferred order type.

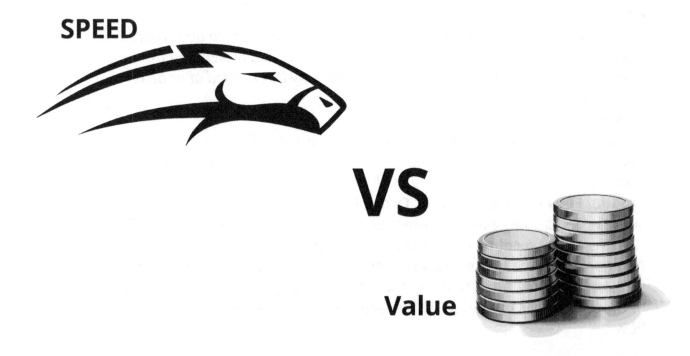

SPEED

VS

Value

Why You Need a Broker for Day Trading

A brokerage, also known as a brokerage firm or a stockbroker, is a financial institution or a company that facilitates the buying and selling of financial securities such as stocks, bonds, options, and mutual funds on behalf of its clients. They act as intermediaries between individual investors and the financial markets.

• Brokerage firms provide individual investors access to the financial markets where securities are bought and sold. They have established relationships with stock exchanges and other market participants, allowing them to execute trades on your behalf.

• Financial markets are regulated to protect investors and maintain the integrity of the trading process. Brokerage firms are licensed and regulated entities that must adhere to specific rules and regulations set by regulatory authorities. They help ensure that your trades comply with applicable laws and regulations.

• Brokerages provide you with an account to hold your investments. This account serves as a centralized platform to manage your portfolio, track your trades, and monitor your investment performance. Like a bank account, you can deposit funds into your account and use them to make investments and buy stocks or withdraw the funds when desired.

• Many brokerage firms offer additional services such as investment advice, research reports, market analysis and educational resources from licensed financial advisors. They can provide insights, recommendations, and guidance on investment opportunities to help you make more informed trading decisions.

• Brokerage firms typically offer user-friendly online trading platforms and mobile apps that make it convenient to place trades, monitor your investments, and access account information. They provide customer support to address any inquiries, or technical difficulties you may encounter.

It's worth noting that while brokerage firms provide valuable services, they may charge fees or commissions for executing trades, managing your account, or providing additional services. The specific fee structure varies, so it's important to research and compare different firms to find one that aligns with your trading needs and preferences.

Day Traders and Scalpers typically look for brokerage services that have little to no fees or commissions to allow the opportunity to make many trades a day for little cost.

Deciding on a Brokerage Account

When opening an account, the broker you choose will ask questions to determine if you are a professional or non-professional trader. Unless you are licensed, you are a non-professional.
Your brokerage will also offer two types of accounts: Cash or Margin.

A Cash Account has no leveraging power, unlike a margin account are not subjected to the PDT rule. Therefore, the total amount you can trade will equal whatever cash you have in your account. It will take 1 days for each trade to settle before the funds are available in your account to trade again. For some day traders, having to wait 1 days can be very difficult.

A Margin Account requires a margin agreement. While it will still take 2 days for the cash in the trade to settle, the broker gives you credit to trade with the money as though it was already settled.

Day traders generally use margin accounts to make multiple trades in a single day. Most margin accounts leverage 4 times your account balance enabling you to invest in much larger share sizes for each trade.

When trading in a margin account you are limited by the PDT Rule. This rule states that if a trader makes more than 3 day trades within 5 business days, they are a day trader and they must maintain a minimum account balance of $25,000.00 USD.

Day Trading involves making a round trip, buying and selling equities in the same day. For example, if you buy 500 shares in a day and sell a portion or all of the shares in the same day you have made a round trip. On the other hand, if you buy or sell shares in a day, maintain all the shares overnight and buy or sell the same shares the next day, you have not made a day trade (or round trip) and this would not count against your maximum of 3 trades in 5 business days.

If you break the PDT rule by executing a 4th trade, you will be flagged as a Pattern Day Trader. Your broker can give you 1 warning (pass). A second violation will result in your account being frozen for 90 days or until your account is brought up to a minimum of $25,000.00 USD. Therefore, it is important to be clear with your broker as to what type of trading you want to do so they can best help you.

Opening a Margin Account and Following the PDT Rule VS Opening an Account Outside the U.S.

Many offshore (outside the U.S.) brokers and platforms do not enforce the PDT Rule. At the time of publication the following are some of the popular offshore brokers' platforms. Most offer margin, some as much as 6 times your account size. However, remember that the PDT rule was created for your protection and trading outside the U.S. comes with additional risks. Ask your licensed financial advisor advice before you commit to a broker.

CMEG -- (Sterling Pro & DAS Trader Pro)
Coinexx -- (MetaTrader 4, MetaTrader 5, cTrader)
NinjaTrader -- (NinjaTrader 8)
IG -- (IG Trading Platform, MetaTrader 4)
Roboforex -- (MetaTrader 4, Metatrader 5, cTrader)
TradeZero -- (TradeZero Pro, DAS Trader Pro)

At the time of publication the following are some of the commonly used U.S. brokerages with platforms that support scalping and day trading, following the PDT rule for the protection of traders.

Ally Invest -- (Ally Invest Live)
ATC Brokers -- (MetaTrader 4 and ATC Trader)
CMC Markets -- (CMC Markets Next Generation)
CenterPoint Securites -- (Sterling Trader Pro, DAS Trader Pro, RealTick Pro)
Charles Schwab & TD Ameritrade -- (thinkorswim)
Cobra Trading -- (Sterling Trader Pro, DAS Trading Pro)
E*TRADE -- (E*TRADE Pro)
Fidelity Investments -- (Active Trader Pro)
First Trade -- (Firstrade Navigator)
Interactive Brokers -- (IBKR TWS)
Lightspeed -- (Lightspeed Trader, Sterling Trader Pro)
Merril Edge -- (Merrill Edge MarketPro)
OANDA -- (OANDA Trade, OANDA MT4/MT5)
SpeedTrader -- (SpeedTrader PRO)
TastyTrades -- (tastyworks)
TradeStation -- (TradeStation 10)
Webull -- (Webull)

Sample of a Typical Brokerage Account Application

When filing for an account to trade with a brokerage, you will often be required to provide the following standard information:

1. Personal Information
   - Full name
   - Date of birth
   - Social Security number (or equivalent identification number)
   - Citizenship or residency status
   - Contact information (address, phone number, email)
2. Employment Information
   - Current occupation
   - Employer's name and address
   - Job title or position
   - Annual income
   - Net worth (total assets minus total liabilities)
3. Financial Information
   - Bank account details (routing number and account number)
   - Investment objectives (e.g., growth income capital preservation)
   - Risk tolerance (e.g., conservative, moderate, aggressive)
4. Trading Experience
   - Previous trading experience (if any)
   - Types of securites traded (stocks, options, futures, etc.)
   - Frequency of trades
   - Average trade size
5. Regulatory Requirements
   - Anti-money laundering (AML) information such as the source of funds and expected transaction volume
   - Declaration of political exposure or public office held
6. Additional Documentation
   - Identification documents (e.g., passport, driver's license, ID card)
   - Proof of address (e.g., utility bill, bank statement)
   - Tax-related documents (e.g., W-9 form in the United States)

The specific requirements may vary depending on the brokerage and the jurisdiction in which you are applying. Some brokerages may require additional information or documentation based on their internal policies or regulatory obligations.

Refresh Your Skills of the Candlestick Patterns and Their Ratings with
the CANDLESTICK PATTERN PLAYBOOK
(DAY TRADING VOL 2)

What's Inside

- Unique Candlestick Pattern Rating System
- The Important Candlestick Patterns You Should Know
- Understand Candlestick Patterns for any Trading Style
- Quizzes and Games to Help Learn Candlestick Patterns
- Flashcards to Help Remember Candlestick Patterns

"Mastering candlestick patterns is the key to profitable trading"
- John Bull Bear

THE CANDLESTICK PATTERN PLAYBOOK

DAY TRADING VOL 2

DAY TRADING VOL 2
A Professional Trader's Guide to Success

THE CANDLESTICK PATTERN PLAYBOOK

Memorize Candlestick Patterns with Charts • Puzzles • Games • Flashcards

DAY TRADING your way to Fast Profits

72.8% Accurate

DOWN TREND

UP TREND

Dragonfly Candle

Understanding a Basic Candlestick is Important to Your Success When Trading the Opening 90 mins

A Basic Candlestick

A basic candlestick represents the price action within a specific time frame, such as a minute, hour, or day. It consists of four main components: open, close, high, and low prices. The body of the candlestick represents the range between the open and close prices, while the wicks or shadows depict the high and low prices.

To trade a single candlestick on an intraday chart, it is important to consider the context and the specific type of candlestick formation. Different candlestick patterns provide insights into market sentiment and potential trading opportunities. For example, a bullish candlestick with a large body and small or nonexistent wicks suggests strong buying pressure. In this case, traders may consider entering a long position or holding onto existing long positions, anticipating further upward movement.

A bearish candlestick with a large body and minimal wicks indicates strong selling pressure. Traders might consider shorting the stock or closing existing long positions to take advantage of potential downward movement.

It is essential to remember that trading decisions should not rely solely on single candlestick formations. It's advisable to use candlestick patterns in conjunction with other indicators, such as moving averages, trendlines, and volume analysis, to confirm potential trade setups and manage risk effectively.

Bullish Candlestick	Bearish Candlestick

Bullish Candlestick

High Price

Upper Wick or Shadow

Closing Price

Body

Opening Price

Lower Wick or Shadow

Low Price

Bearish Candlestick

High Price

Upper Wick or Shadow

Opening Price

Body

Closing Price

Lower Wick or Shadow

Low Price

Refresh Your Skills with Candlestick Mastery Beginner to Pro in 66 Patterns (DAY TRADING VOL 3)

"Candlestick Mastery Beginner to Pro in 66 Patterns" is an engaging guide that hones your technical analysis skills through a series of hands-on exercises. With challenges ranging from recognizing named candlestick patterns to predicting their direction, this book offers a dynamic learning experience, culminating in the ultimate test of naming the patterns.

Challenges Include:

• Beginner: Find the Named Candlestick Patterns
• Advanced: Find and Name the Candlestick Patterns
• Expert: Name and Predict the Direction of the Candlestick Pattern
• Professional: Name the Candlestick Patterns

Course and Study Guide for
"The Candlestick Pattern Playbook"

Candlestick Mastery Beginner to Pro in 66 Patterns

DAY TRADING VOL 3

Learn Technical Analysis with
Charts and Challenges

Candlestick Mastery Beginner to Pro
in 66 Patterns

DAY TRADING VOL 3

17th century Munehisa Homma contemplates his next trade

This image provided by John Bull Bear historical archives was created shortly after the disastrous abacus accident that cost Munehisa his ring finger. Some believe the accident caused the mathematical error that triggered the catastrophic rice shortage of 1687 which resulted in many citizens losing their life savings.

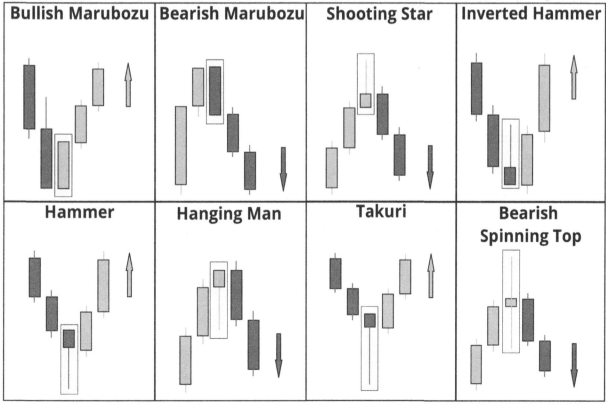

| Bullish Marubozu | Bearish Marubozu | Shooting Star | Inverted Hammer |
| Hammer | Hanging Man | Takuri | Bearish Spinning Top |

CHAPTER 2

DO YOU HAVE WHAT IT TAKES TO TRADE THE OPEN?

Mastering the Market Open

Trading the market open is a favored strategy among many day traders for several compelling reasons. This period is marked by heightened volatility and increased liquidity in price action from the minute the bell rings as the accumulation of overnight news and economic data influences market sentiment. Traders will often capitalize on these dynamics, seeking to profit from significant price movements that frequently occur during the first few minutes to hour after the market opens.

One popular appoach involves trading based on catalysts such as earnings reports, geopolitical events, or economic indicators released just before the open. These events can create immediate and substantial impacts on stock prices, offering opportunities for traders to buy high and sell higher as the market reacts. The strategy hinges on anticipating how the market will interpret and respond to the news, thus making quick decisions crucial at the open.

A common technique is to focus on the short term price action of the opening candle on one-minute charts. Traders look for patterns or price levels set by this initial activity to make predictions about subsequent movements. This method appeals to those who prefer technical analysis over fundamental analysis, relying on quick, short-term gains based on observed price behaviors rather than underlying economic conditions.

Despite the potential for rapid profits, trading the open carries considerable risks. The same volatility that can provide substantial returns can also lead to significant losses, especially if traders do not have solid risk management strategies in place. The fast-paced environment of the opening market can also fuel an adrenaline rush that some traders find addictive, treating trading more like a game than a strategic financial activity. This mindset can be dangerous, as it may encourage taking excessive risks or trading impulsively without a well-thought-out plan.

The following strategies will outline 4 different ways to trade the open. These strategies capitalize on the volatility and directional momentum that occur when specific price thresholds set during the pre-market and early market hours are crossed. Each of these strategies serves different trading styles and risk tolerances, from aggressive, quick scalps to more measured, short-term trades. Traders often choose a strategy based on their personal risk appetite, trading goals, and the specific market conditions of the day. Each will be futher explained throughout this book.

The 4 Open Strategies

Strategy 1: Pre-Market High and Low Levels

This strategy involves marking the highest and lowest price points of the candlestick **bodies** that the stock reaches between 7:30 AM and 9:15 AM ET, during the pre-market trading session on the New York Stock Exchange on a **5-minute chart.** Traders watch these levels closely at the market open. A move above or below these pre-market levels typically indicates a stong directional momentum, prompting traders to enter long or short positions accordingly. The rationale is that breaking these levels suggests a trend or a continutation of buying or selling interest. Do not mark the last 15 minutes of the pre-market as part of the breakout levels. These final minutes, due to their increased volatility, often will not reflect the true breakout range of the stock.

Strategy 2: Last 30-Minute Candle Pre-Market

For this strategy, traders mark the high and low of the last 30 minute candle's **body** that closes at 9:00 AM ET, just before the regular market session begins on a **30-minute chart**. This approach assumes that the final movements in the pre-market are predicting a range of consolidating price action during the first hour after the market opens. If price action breaks these levels it signifies a possible trend and the entry of a trade.

Strategy 3: First 5-Minute Candle Range Post-Open

This strategy focuses on the first 5-minute candle after the market officially opens. By marking the high and low of this candle's **body**, on a **5-minute chart** traders set definitive thresholds for measuring the initial market reaction. A break above or below this range can be considered a strong indicator of the immediate market trend. This method is highly reactive and requires quick decision-making to capitalize on the swift moves typical of the first 30 minutes after the opening bell.

Strategy 4: First 15-Minute Candle Range Post-Open

Similar to the previous strategy, this strategy extends the observation window to the first 15 minutes of trading, providing a broader view of the market's opening behavior. By marking the high and low of the 15-minute candle's **body**, on a **15-minute chart** traders can gauge the early market momentum with slightly more data , potentially reducing the noise and false signals common in shorter time frames. A breakout of this range is used to signal longer-lasting moves, which might be more reliable but could have less explosive initial momentum compared to the 5-minute strategy.

Implementing the Strategies

For each strategy, once a level range is breached, traders enter trades in the direction of the breakout, aiming to capitalize on the continued momentum. Profit targets are based on historical pivot points and other significant price levels identified from up to 10 days of prior price action set on a 5-minute chart. Stops are based on maximum loss per trade or if the price retraces half of the previous 1-minute candle.

Please Note: Times are based on U.S. Eastern Time Zone (ET)

Trading the Open is not for Everyone.
Do you have the Right Stuff?

If you're trading the Open, you need to be able to think fast and have an understanding of market price movements. Those with certain careers or different training can make it look simple while others may struggle or even fail. It is important to test your skills in a simulator before you trade with real money at the Open.

Are Gamers the new Trading Millionaires?

Why Gamers or People who Work Under High Stress and Fast-Paced Careers Have an Edge

In recent years, a fascinating trend has emerged within the world of day trading, in that many of its most successful practitioners are those who have a background in video gaming. This chapter explores why individuals who frequently play video games may find themselves well equipped for the high speed, high stakes environment of scalping in the stock market, while also cautioning against treating financial markets like just another game.

The Gaming Connection
From Gaming Controllers to Scalping with Hotkeys

Enhanced Hand-Eye Coordination and Reflexes

Video gaming from a young age cultivates exceptional hand-eye coordination and quick reflexes. These skills are directly transferable to scalping, where traders must react swiftly to rapidly changing price action. The ability to process visual information quickly and respond almost instantaneously gives gamers a significant edge in executing trades at the most opportune moments.

Strategic Thinking and Decision-Making

Advanced video games often require complex strategic thinking and the ability to make decisions quickly under pressure. These capabilities are invaluable in scalping, where success depends on making numerous fast-paced decisions based on the analysis of real time financial data.

Risk Management

Just as gamers must manage resources and assess risk reward scenarios in their gameplay, traders need to evaluate the risks and potential benefits of their trades carefully. Gamers often develop an innate sense for managing these balances, which can translate into effective financial decision making

Emotional Control

Successful gaming requires emotional control to prevent tilt, a term used in gaming to describe a scenario where a player becomes visibly frustrated and performs poorly. Similarly in trading, emotional control is critical to maintaining discipline and sticking to a predetermined trading strategy, especially in the volatile realm of scalping.

Not Just Another Game

When Trading Becomes Just Another Game

While the skills developed through gaming can provide a foundational advantage, there are significant risks when traders treat the stock market as a game rather than a serious financial endeavor. Often, there are no trades to take at all, and gamers have a hard time just not playing the "game" anyway.

Overconfidence
Gamers used to dominating in a virtual arena may bring an overconfident mindset to trading, assuming they can easily conquer the market. This overconfidence can lead to taking excessive risks and neglecting the importance of being disciplined and following a trading plan or strategy.

The Illusion of Control
Video games often give players the illusion of control over the outcome, which is not the case in the unpredicatable stock market. Recognizing and accounting for the elements of trading that cannot be controlled is crucial for long-term success.

Game-like Engagement
The exciting, fast-paced nature of scalping can be particularly appealing for practiced gamers. However, without strict discipline, this can lead to over-trading or trading for excitement rather then profit, mirroring the compulsion to play 'just one more game."

Bridging the Gap: Turning Gaming Skills into Trading Success

To leverage their gaming skills effectively, traders who are gamers should focus on education and comprehensive training in a simulator offered by their broker's platform, which will ultimately serve for their live trading. Choosing a broker with a good simulator program is essential.

Developing a Trading Plan
Just as a gamer develops strategies to tackle different levels or opponents, traders should develop detailed trading plans that included entry and exit strategies, risk management techniques, and criteria for selecting trades.

Gamers that transition their gaming skills into a profitable living, correctly adjust their mindset and understand that trading is not a game but a serious financial activity that requires a professional attitude toward potential losses and gains.

CHAPTER 3

**Do you Know Yourself?
Can you Control Your Emotions
and Manage Your Risk?**

Who Am I?

Change How You Think and Feel

Trading in the stock market is not like anything else one prepares for in life. In almost any other endeavour, a person can either manipulate or change the rules in the middle of a personal challenge. In other words, rewrite the script at anytime to help come to terms with a less than positive result. This can help or hurt us in our life journey, depending on the circumstances and actual goals. This type of mindset in trading can lead to financial ruin. The market has endless probabilities that cannot be calculated by the human mind and a trader should always be prepared for their trade to go against them.

There are no life training lessons to prepare us for the random aspect of the stock market. We take the lessons we know and try to apply them into an unforgiving random set of circumstances that cannot be manipulated or changed for our benefit no matter how much we believe we can change things to go our way. In almost every way, our past experiences set us up to fail at trading. Overcoming these past lessons is the key to success in becoming a good trader. Understanding that you have no control is the key and is almost impossible for new traders to accept.

Good traders need to come to terms with the emotional challenges of day trading and scalping. One of the most significant emotional hurdles for traders is the transition from early successes, often driven by luck. Many beginners experience a period of initial success that can create unrealistic expectations about the ease and profitability of trading. However, as the market's complexity becomes more apparent, these traders often find their early strategies unworkable over the long term, leading to frustration and doubt.

This transition phase is crucial because it is where many traders confront the reality of the trading profession; it is not merely about making profitable trades, but managing losses as well. The realization that not all trades will be winners and that losses are part of the game can be a hard pill to swallow. This leads to the first major challenge: Dealing with loss. Losses in trading can evoke strong emotional responses, primarily fear and regret and even anger, which can cloud judgment and lead to erratic trading behavior, like revenge trading - where a trader tries to recover losses quickly without a solid strategy thinking they can somehow control the market to bend their way.

This often leads to a crossroads and the reality they must confront. No one really knows what price direction a stock will move. Good traders prepare themselves for losses and the random possibility of every trade. Plan on a loss first, when making a trading plan. Can you accept that amount of loss? If you can't, your share size may be too high.

Understanding Risk Managment

Day trading risk management refers to the strategies and techniques employed by traders to control and mitigate the potential risk associated with their trading activities. Scalping involves buying and selling financial instruments within minutes or seconds, aiming to profit from short-term price movements and can be a highly volatile and risky endeavor. Effective risk management is crucial to protect capital and maintain profitability.

Some short term scalpers determine their potential profit (reward) and loss (risk) for each trade they take. Most aim to maintain a favorable risk-reward ratio, where the potential reward out weighs the potential risk. By setting a defined ratio, such as 2:1, traders often try to ensure that their winning trades can offset their losing trades.

It is important to follow your day trading plan and have a maximum stop loss per trade predetermined before you enter a trade. This helps limit potential losses by ensuring the positions are closed before losses become excessive. The best price level to set a stop-loss should be clearly defined prior to entering a trade as per the strategy you are following.

Scalpers also carefully determine the appropriate position size for each trade based on risk tolerance and the specific trade setup. Position sizing involves calculating the number of shares, taking into account factors like account size, risk per trade, and stop-loss level. Proper position sizing ensures comfort and an option to stay in the move through additional potential profit levels.

Some day traders will allocate a specific portion of their total capital as risk capital, which is the amount they are willing to risk on day trading and scalping activities. By separating risk capital from other funds, such as long-term investments or living expenses, traders protect themselves from severe financial consequences in case of losses.

The open strategies are unique and use historical price levels that have been identified on charts to decide profit taking levels. They typically do not use a risk/reward ratio. They exit a trade at profit pivot levels and use recent price action to determine the exit of a losing trade. **The open strategies typically call for an exit of a losing trade as the price action retraces half of the previous 1-minute candle or reaches your maximum loss per trade.**

Why do 95% of all Traders Fail?

Many successful traders use **fundamental analysis** by studying the strength of a company to pick their stocks to trade while others use technical analysis to pick their stocks by studying historical data.

The most successful day traders and scalpers have also learned to understand their own emotions with **mental analysis**. The traders that can control themselves and follow their trading plan, day after day without fail, are often the most successful traders in the market.

Trading the open uses a **combination of mental and technical analysis**. Once you have studied the strategies within this book, the *real* job is to create a trading plan you can follow and then putting in the time to understanding *yourself*. Trading plans can be made easily enough, but the discipline to follow them is the real issue for most traders and why so many fail.

It makes no difference if a person is highly educated and successful in business. Some of the best traders have almost no education, while those well educated and successful in other ways can fail badly at trading. Often, doing well in school or other walks of life does not benefit you in a trading career because it has not prepared you for a mindset of thinking in probabilites This is why following a plan is key and the most important factor to become successful in scalping the open.

Once you understand that any trade can go against you at any time you will have crossed a major hurdle that holds back so many traders from becoming successful. No matter how good a trade looks and how well its data lines up with your research there will always be a strong probability it will not react the way you think. This is why professional traders look at longer time frames to assess their level of success. They stick to the plan, win or lose, keeping their losses small and riding the winners for all they can get. They try to take the emotion out of short term losses and focus on the big picture and an overall winning average.

If you have difficulty admitting you can be wrong at least 50% of the time, you will struggle to become profitable. Understanding that you will fail a large percentage of the time can free you from trading depression swings and worse, revenge trading causing much larger losses than your trading plan provides for.

It can't be said enough. **THIS IS THE KEY:** Detach yourself from wins or losses and trade the plan and *only* the plan. Believe in yourself, trust your day trading plan and move foward with slow confidence. Study and trade your strategies in a simulator until they are proven, then if you can also master your emotions, you have a chance of becoming one of the 5% that succeed in day trading.

Handling the Emotional Toll

The emotional toll of repeated losses can be debilitating. Continuous negative outcomes can lead to a decline in confidence, second-guessing one's decisions, and in some cases, complete withdrawal from trading activities. This is often exacerbated by the solitude many traders experience, as trading can be a lonely endeavor without the immediate camaraderie of a traditional work place.

The key to overcoming these emotional challenges lies in developing a robust trading plan and a mindset that accepts losses as an integral part of trading. A well-thought-out trading plan helps maintain focus and provides a framework that can bring a sense of control and order to strategies, such as setting stop-loss orders and having rules for when to exit a trade, both in profit and loss situations.

Building Emotional Resilience

Building emotional resilience is essential for long-term success in trading. This involves training oneself to detach from the outcomes of individual trades and focus on the overall trading process and performance. Mindfulness and meditation can be effective tools for managing stress and keeping emotions in check. Setting realistic expectations is crucial. Understanding that trading is not a get-rich-quick scheme but a serious business with risks, can help set a more balanced emotional outlook. Reflecting on one's trades regularly to learn from mistakes and successes alike can help refine strategies and build confidence.

Support Systems and Continuous Learning

Having a support system such as trading communities or mentors, can also provide emotional relief and valuable insights. Sharing experiences with fellow traders can alleviate the sense of isolation and provide new perspectives on handling losses and emotional stress. Continuous learning and adaption are also crucial in the ever-evolving markets. Traders who invest time in learning from each trade, stay updated with market trends and refine their strategies, tend to find better success and emotional stability.

The emotional journey of a trader is fraught with challenges, but also opportunities for personal growth and professional development. By accepting that losses are a natural part of trading, adopting a disciplined approach to risk management, and continuously striving to improve one's skills and strategies, traders can navigate the emotional highs and lows more effectively. Embracing these principles can not only lead to better trading outcomes but contribute to more satisfying and sustainable trading career.

Ten Rules that All Traders Should Follow

1. Develop a Trading Plan. Create a comprehensive trading plan that includes entry and exit strategies, risk management techniques, and profit targets. This plan serves as a guide to prevent emotional decision-making during trading.

2. Set Realistic Expectations. Understand that losses are part of trading and set realistic expectations for winning and losing. This helps prevent disappointment and emotional responses to normal market fluctuations.

3. Practice Risk Management. Always know how much you are willing to lose on a trade and set stop-loss orders to manage this risk. This prevents emotional fallout from unexpectedly large losses.

4. Maintain Discipline. Stick to your trading plan and strategies, even when tempted by potential quick gains or swayed by fear. Discipline helps you stay the course and protects against emotional trading.

5. Keep Emotions in Check. Recognize personal emotional triggers that may lead you to make impulsive decisions. Use techniques such as deep breathing, taking breaks, or even meditation to maintain emotional equilibrium.

6. Use a Trading Journal. Keep a record of all trades, including the emotional state during each trade, to identify patterns in emotional responses that effect trading performance. Reflect on these and learn how to improve.

7. Review and Reflect. Regularly review your trades to assess both successful and unsuccessful decisions. Learning from mistakes helps improve strategies and reduce emotional mistakes in the future.

8. Limit Exposure. Don't overexpose yourself to the market. Trading too frequently or risking too much can heighten emotional responses. Find a balance that keeps you calm and focused.

9. Educate Yourself. Continuous learning about the markets, trading techniques, and financial management helps build confidence, reducing the anxiety and fear associated with trading.

10. Support Network. Engage with a community of traders or a mentor. Sharing experiences and gaining insights from others can provide emotional support and reduce the feeling of isolation that many traders experience.

By integrating these points into your trading practice, you can better manage your emotions, leading to more rational decision-making and improved trading outcomes.

Master Simulated Trading

Most platforms offer a simulator that utilizes their charts and trading tools. This is known as paper trading. It is very important to become successful in a simulator before you trade the **Open Strategy** (or any strategy) live, with real money.

If your platform doesn't offer some type of simulator it is highly advisable to find one that does. This is one of the most important steps toward success.

Follow your trading plan in the simulator as if your funds were real. Log your trades and your thought process for each trade to guide improvement. Make sure the share size you trade in the simulator is the same amount of funds you are actually willing to risk.

Simulators can be very helpful and are a useful tool in improving your trading. Many beginning traders do not take them seriously while trading with them and have difficulty making the transition to live trading. If you do not stick to your risk management and share size plan as if you were trading with real funds, you risk failure when you transition to live trading with real funds.

Fear of losing takes control of what otherwise may have been a very good entry or exit within the Open strategy and can be a common downfall. Emotions spell the doom of most day traders. All traders are affected by them to some extent. Trade in a simulator until you are profitable for many months and then when you go live, to be extra safe, lower your share size until your live trading is also successful for many months.

I'm waiting to finish this book and have success in a stock trading simulator using the trading plan, daily guidelines and trading logs supplied.

A WINNER

There's no time, we're losing so much money by waiting, we got this!

UM....... NOT WINNERS

Suggested Trading Plan Criteria

Trading Hours:	
Entry Share Size:	
Min Profit per Trade:	
Max Loss per Trade:	
Daily Goal:	
Max Loss per Day:	
Notes:	

Your Trading Plan

CHAPTER 4

Layout and Tools

Your Trading Layout

Creating an efficient trading layout is crucial for scalpers, especially when navigating the fast-paced environment of the market open. An effective layout not only provides immediate access to necessary data but also aids in rapid decision-making, which is essential for executing successful trades within brief time windows. This chapter covers a layout designed by professional traders showing the tools you will need to optimize it for various strategies, focusing on essential elements such as the Volume Profile, Level II data, intraday charting tools, time and sales, candlestick patterns, multiple chart time frame setups and more.

Your Broker should offer you all the tools you need to build your own layout to help you trade. It is important they have these available tools so you can take fast trades in order to capitalize on the Open Strategies.

Speed is Important

This is a Typical Layout for the Open Strategy

① One-minute chart with the Volume Profile and the Million-Dollar Margin Club Scalping Indicator

② Time and Sales -Often used to show volatility and sentiment of the stock being traded

③ Level II - Used to judge the direction of the stock based on open   orders on the Bid & Ask

④ 5-minute chart with RSI and MACD oscillator studies

⑤ Active Trader - Tool for placing and monitoring trades (the Ladder is hidden)

⑥ 5-minute chart

⑦ Daily chart*

⑧ 5-minute set to monitor the SPY*

⑨ Daily News*

Many of the charts are minimized for screen management

Most of the focus when trading this layout is in the following order of importance:

1-minute chart, Level II, Scalping or volume indicator, and finding possible directional alignment of the 1-minute and 5-minute chart. Some chart time increments are set differently depending on the current trades and the volume profiles.

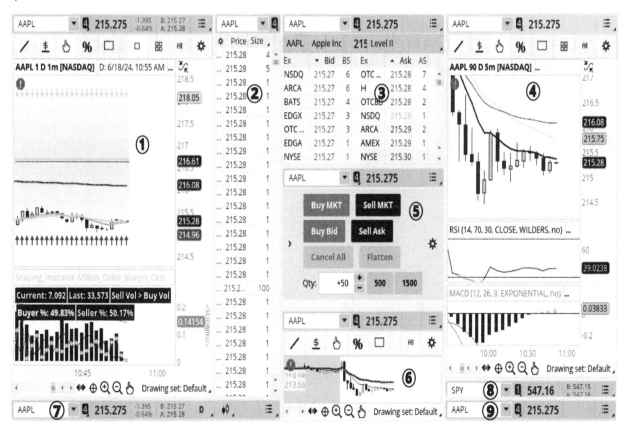

The 7 Essential Trading Tools That Should be on Every Professional Layout

1. Level II Data

2. News Source

3. Trade Order Tool

4. Scanner

5. Time and Sales Data

6. Charts with Candlestick Patterns and Other Indicators

7. Watchlists

1. Level II Data

The diagram on the following page is showing the Level II (**Book**) representing the current value of the stock.

On the left is the **BID** (what potential buyers are willing to pay to purchase a single share). On the right is the **ASK** (what potential sellers are asking others to pay to buy a single share). Bid size (**BS)** represents how many shares potential buyers want to buy. Ask size (**AS)** represents how many shares potential sellers want to sell. **EX** (exchange) represents the marketplaces where stocks are bought and sold.

On most Level II diagrams the **BS** and **AS** only show the partial order quantity. For example, on the diagram on the next page, the true amount of the number of shares that are being offered to buy or sell is calculated by multiplying the numbers in the **BS** or **AS** columns by 100 to get the actual number of shares represented. This may change depending on your setting or broker's platform.

A larger number of shares offered on the BID than the ASK indicates a possible continued price movement upward. A larger number of shares offered on the ASK than the BID indicates a possible continued price movement down.

This level II diagram shows the highest price is $183.40. As you look down the right column (ASK) you can see many shares available at that same price. The first number at the top of the column (24) multiplied by 100 is actually 2400 shares. As you read down the right column the sum of all the shares priced at $183.40 equals 6900 shares.

This is typically considered a large number of shares available at the same price. Often it will take multiple buyers (bidders) to purchase all of these shares. Because there might not be enough buyers (bidders) waiting to purchase these large amount of shares, the movement in the price may be affected for a period of time until they are all purchased. The difference between the number of sellers (ASKS) versus the available buyers (BIDS) may even change the direction of the current price action trend and move the price downward. Often, sellers will want to reduce their asking price to make sure their shares sell. As more and more sellers lower the price of their shares, the overall value of the stock may begin to decrease. Sometimes, this can happen very quickly and change the direction of the stock represented on your chart's candlesticks and price level.

Identifying these larger blocks of shares available at the same price level can be very helpful when deciding whether to enter or exit a position. Typically, but not always, when there are not enough buyers to purchase at the ASK price, the share price drops so that the shares will sell. This can work the opposite way when the BID is stacked up with buyers waiting, driving the price higher.

Level II Data provides a deeper look into the market's order book beyond just the current bid and ask prices. It shows the price levels of open buy and sell orders and is crucial for understanding potential support and resistance levels. Having Level II data prominently displayed on your layout allows you to gauge the depth of the market, helping anticipate short term price moves based on where orders are clustered.

Example of Level II

Difference in price between Bid and Ask (Spread)

Exchange	Buyer's Price	Shares= BS x 100	Exchange	Seller's Price	Shares= AS x 100
Ex	▼ Bid	BS	Ex	▲ Ask	AS
NSDQ	183.39	3	EDGX	183.40	24
ARCA	183.38	5	OTCBB	183.40	19
BATS	183.38	4	NSDQ	183.40	10
EDGX	183.38	3	NYSE	183.40	5
H	183.38	1	ARCA	183.40	5
NYSE	183.38	1	BATS	183.40	3
OTCBB	183.38	1	EDGA	183.40	2
OTC ...	183.38	1	H	183.40	1
PHLX	183.37	1	OTC ...	183.41	1
BSE	183.32	1	PHLX	183.41	1
CHXE	183.32	1	CHXE	183.46	1
Y	183.32	1	BSE	183.47	1
CINN	183.08	1	Y	183.50	1
EDGA	182.79	1	CINN	183.66	1
ETMM	182.79	1	ETMM	183.71	1
AMEX	181.64	1	AMEX	184.00	1

As seen in DAY TRADING VOL 1

2. News Source

The News tool on a trading platform is an integrated feature that provides traders with real-time news updates and financial analysis directly within the platform. This tool is essential for staying informed about significant events that can affect market conditions, such as economic indicators, FDA approvals, earnings announcements, regulatory changes, and geopolitical developments. Having access to timely and relevant news allows traders to make more informed decisions and react quickly to market-moving events. This feature often allows for customization, enabling traders to receive news alerts based on specific markets, sectors, or individual securities of interest, thereby aligning with their trading strategies and preferences.

NVDA ▼ 4	Nvidia Corp	**120.88**	-1.10 -0.90%	B: 120.88 A: 120.88	☰

Time ▼	Title (Click for story)
09:00:13	From Nvidia's Stock Split, Intel's Revitalized AI Strategy To T...
05:30:00	Nvidia's New Sales Booster: The Global Push for Domestic ...
6/8/24	Nvidia's Jensen Huang Surpasses Michael Dell In Wealth As ...
6/8/24	MW Tech stocks see biggest weekly inflows in over 2 month...
6/8/24	MW What Nvidia's stock split means for investors
6/8/24	MW Nvidia CEO on work/life balance: 'When I'm not workin...
6/8/24	MW Stock market's records belie the cracks forming beneat...
6/7/24	Apple's AI Strategy Could Trigger Three-Year iPhone Sales B...
6/7/24	The Hottest New Celebrity Is...a Chip CEO -- WSJ
6/7/24	U.S. stocks close slightly lower after jobs data
6/7/24	GameStop slumps as 'Roaring Kitty' returns to YouTube
6/7/24	The Score: Spotify, Nvidia, GameStop and More Stocks That ...
6/7/24	Apple Needs an AI Miracle at WWDC. The Stock Is Counting ...
6/7/24	S&P 500 Posts Weekly Gain Ahead of Fed Meeting as Nvidia...
6/7/24	US Equity Indexes Rise This Week as Nvidia Lifts Technolog...
6/7/24	Stocks Hit Record Highs, Central Banks Cut Rates, Tight US J...
6/7/24	Nvidia Filed Amendment To Effect Stock Split And Proportio...
6/7/24	MW AMD's stock hasn't been feeling the love. Here's why th...
6/7/24	US Markets Briefing: Payrolls data muddies outlook ahe...
6/7/24	Nvidia's AI Chip - The Product Propelling Its Success
6/7/24	Nividia Is Riding AI Chip Demand to Stock Market Glory. Wh...
6/7/24	MW This chart shows Nvidia's meteoric rise as 'Jensenity' c...
6/7/24	Amazon Could Join the $3 Trillion Club. How It Could Happe...
6/7/24	AI Is Still Hot but Investors Are Getting Pickier -- Barrons.com
6/7/24	10 Information Technology Stocks Whale Activity In Today's ...
6/7/24	TSMC-Backed U.S. Fund Targets Chip, Robotics, And Hardwa...
6/7/24	Smart Money Trims Stocks On Strong Jobs Report - Raise H...
6/7/24	Nvidia Stock Split: What Investors Need To Know, What Past...
6/7/24	The Week in Numbers: trillion dollar babies
6/7/24	Trading at Noon: Bumper jobs growth dents September ...
6/7/24	Nvidia Stock Has Left AMD and Intel Behind. One Could Cat...
6/7/24	Industry Comparison: Evaluating NVIDIA Against Competito...
6/7/24	Market Clubhouse Morning Memo - June 7th, 2024 (Trade St...

3. Trade Order Tool

A trading platform tool that provides a way to enter and exit positions quickly and show your open positions with profit or loss amounts in real time is essential. As shown in the example below, vital information is available on the Trading Order Tool to help the trader make quick decisions for the Open Strategy. Depending on what your platform offers, you should find a variety of settings for the Trade Order Tool features.

① Stock Ticker/Symbol
② Stock description
③ Current price of stock
④ Bid and Ask prices of stock
⑤ ETB = Easy To Borrow and HTB = Hard To Borrow
⑥ Current number of shares owned for stock
⑦ Buttons for trade using market or limit orders
⑧ Buttons for canceling, reversing, or flattening a position
⑨ Quantity to be traded when buying or selling
⑩ Quantity to add to quantity being traded
⑪ Template for trading single buy or sell, or bracketed buy and sell
⑫ TIF (Time In Force) for premarket, market, or after-market trading hours
⑬ Auto Send - Check for instant trades with no pop-up trade window
⑭ Trading price, quantity, profit loss for current trade and current day

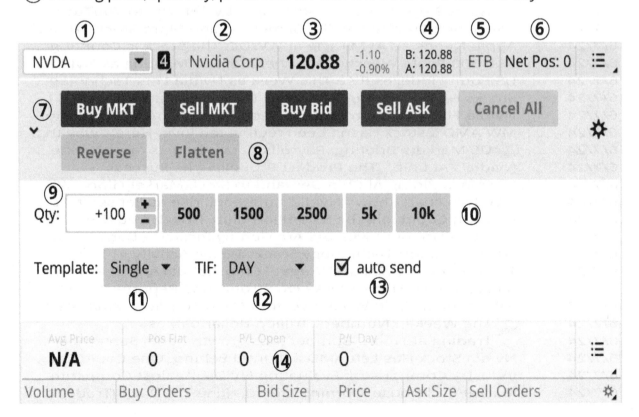

4. Scanner

A Scanner tool on trading platforms helps traders identify short term trading opportunities based on pre-defined criteria or find stocks to add to their watchlist for the day. These criteria can include a variety of technical and volume-related parameters. A scanner monitors the market in real-time, alerting traders to stocks that meet their specified conditions. Below is an example of a scanner with pre-defined settings to find stocks to trade the Open Strategies. Depending on what your platform offers, you should find a variety of settings for your scanner.

① Stock Filter (criteria) for current price of stock

② Custom Study Filter for an ATR that is greater than $4 over 14 days (Bars)

③ Quantity of stocks to scan for

④ Sort by category (Volume)

⑤ Sort the category in order of highest to lowest or lowest to highest

⑥ Scan button to execute a scan for stocks

⑦ Symbol/Stock Ticker

⑧ Last price at which stock was traded

⑨ The percentage of change from the open

⑩ Volume of the shares traded for the day

⑪ Highest price of the day

⑫ Bid price

⑬ Ask price

⑭ Lowest price of the day

⑮ Current ATR

⑯ HTB/ETB = Hard To Borrow or Easy To Borrow

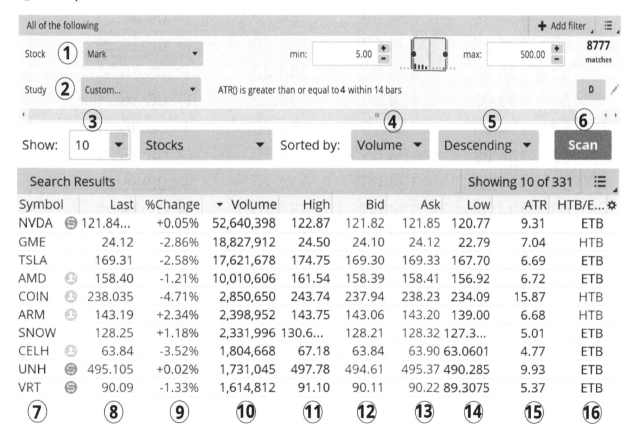

Page 41

5. Time and Sales Data

Also known as the 'tape', the time and sales data shows every transaction that occurs, detailing the time, price, and size of each trade. This real-time data is crucial for scalpers, as it indicates the flow of orders after the sales close from the LVL II and can help confirm movements suggested by other indicators.

DELL	▼	4 131.64	0 0.00%	B: 133.53 A: 133.69	☰

Size	Price	Bid	Ask	X ⚙ ▲	Time
67	134.08	134.00	134.16	P	08:36:21
35	134.08	134.00	134.16	Q	08:36:21
34	134.12	134.00	134.20	P	08:36:21
67	134.08	134.00	134.20	Q	08:36:21
34	134.08	134.00	134.20	K	08:36:21
34	134.07	134.00	134.20	K	08:36:21
67	134.08	134.00	134.20	Q	08:36:21
67	134.08	134.00	134.20	P	08:36:21
67	134.08	134.00	134.20	Q	08:36:21
67	134.08	134.00	134.20	P	08:36:21
67	134.08	134.00	134.20	Q	08:36:21
67	134.08	134.00	134.20	P	08:36:21
67	134.08	134.00	134.20	Q	08:36:21
67	134.08	134.00	134.20	P	08:36:21
67	134.08	134.00	134.20	Q	08:36:21
67	134.08	134.00	134.20	P	08:36:21
67	134.08	134.00	134.20	P	08:36:21
67	134.08	134.00	134.20	Q	08:36:21
10	134.10	134.00	134.20	K	08:36:22
153	134.04	134.00	134.20	D	08:36:24
100	134.06	134.00	134.20	P	08:36:24
1	134.05	134.00	134.20	P	08:36:24
34	134.04	134.00	134.20	P	08:36:24
7	134.04	134.00	134.20	P	08:36:24

The time and sales data, also know as the "T&S" or "tape," is a trading tool that provides a chronological record of most trades executed for a particular security. It displays the price, quantity, and time of each individual trade that goes through an exchange, which allows traders to analyze the buying and selling activity in real-time.

The time and sales ticker provides information on the volume of trades for a specific security. Traders can also analyze the size of trades to gauge the level of liquidity and market interest in the security. Higher trade volumes and larger trade sizes may indicate increased market activity and potentially more reliable price movements.

By observing whether trades are predominantly occurring at the bid or ask prices, traders can infer the overall market sentiment. If a majority of trades are happening at the bid price, it suggests selling pressure or bearish sentiment. If trades are mostly taking place at the ask price, it indicates buying interest or bullish sentiment. Monitoring the trade direction in real-time can help traders assess the balance between supply and demand.

The time and sales ticker also provides information on the speed at which trades are occurring. Rapid succession of trades at similar prices may indicate increased momentum or a potential price trend. Traders can look for patterns in trade execution speed and use this information to identify potential entry or exit points for their trading strategies.

The time and sales data allows traders to analyze the sequence of trades and identify patterns in the order flow. By examining the price, quantity, and timing of trades, traders gain insights into the behavior of participants. For example, large trades executed at or near the bid or ask price may indicate institutional or significant retail trader activity, potentially influencing price movement.

The T&S ticker can also help identify support and resistance levels based on trade execution patterns. Traders look for price levels where a significant number of trades occur or where large trade sizes are executed. These levels act as areas of buying or selling interest, potentially influencing future price movements. Often, prior levels can be utilized to confirm profit levels for the open stratgies.

6. Charts with Candlestick Patterns and Other Indicators

There are hundreds of indicators that scalpers can use to help them determine entries and exits. Each trader will need to determine what works best for them with the strategy that they are using. The professional layouts included in this book will give you some ideas on what others use to scalp the Open Strategies effectively.

Candlestick Patterns on your chart are fundamental to your trading, offering visual insight into market sentiment and potential reversals, that allow you to see the historical price movemnet of a stock and help you create your profit levels for the Open Strategies.

During the COVID-19 pandemic, millions of people were stuck at home and ventured into day trading and scalping. This influx of traders helped to increase the accuracy of all patterns, making patterns that were previously only considered for day charts more reliable for intraday charts as well. This phenomenon is commonly referred to as the Pandemic Pattern Phenomenon (PPP); often described as traders creating a 'self-fulfilling prophecy'. This means that more traders reacting to a pattern in a certain way, make that pattern react accordingly. This has become a vital tool used by short term scalpers, and is described in more detail in the best selling books, **Day Trading Vol 2 (The Candlestick Pattern Playbook)** and **Day Trading Vol 3 (Candlestick Mastery Beginner to Pro in 66 Patterns.)**

Example of a Chart with Candlestick Patterns and Volume

7. Watchlists

A watchlist on trading platforms is a critical feature that allows traders to monitor and track specific stocks. Adding stocks of interest to their watchlist assists traders in keeping a close eye on real-time price movements, updates, and key market data for selected assets. This tool enhances trading efficiency by organizing potential stocks to trade in one accessible location, enabling quick analysis and decision making. Watchlists often include customizable alerts, which help traders act swiftly according to their trading strategy and ensure that they never miss critical trading opportunities. Your watchlist is a great place to start when you are assessing stocks to trade at the open.

Symbol		Last	Net Chng	Bid	Ask	▾ ATR	HTB/ETB
COIN		244.16	-12.92	244.60	244.99	16.04	HTB
CRWD		349.12	+8.63	367.80	367.89	14.57	ETB
META	Ⓢ	492.96	-.80	492.25	492.90	11.94	ETB
LULU		317.86	-5.17	317.50	318.25	10.79	ETB
CRM		241.85	-.91	241.55	243.43	9.51	ETB
DELL		129.97	-3.99	128.83	129.00	9.46	ETB
CEG		198.00	-4.60	197.25	198.50	9.41	ETB
GEV		162.08	+1.77	161.45	162.79	7.65	ETB
GME		28.22	-18.33	27.11	27.16	7.51	HTB
MSFT		423.85	-.67	423.60	423.85	7.15	ETB
AMD		167.87	+1.09	167.45	167.50	6.77	ETB
TSLA		177.48	-.46	177.47	177.50	6.76	ETB
ENPH		122.75	-9.55	122.40	122.73	6.5	ETB
CVNA		106.56	+1.89	106.00	106.60	6.18	HTB
QCOM		206.62	-2.82	206.01	206.50	5.83	ETB
PDD		143.90	+.07	143.65	143.70	5.71	ETB
VRT	Ⓢ	87.68	-.32	87.60	88.35	5.68	ETB
VST	Ⓢ	85.07	-1.19	83.90	86.00	5.65	ETB
SNOW		131.21	-.83	130.65	131.40	5.08	ETB
NVDA	Ⓢ	120.88	-1.10	120.88	120.88	4.55	ETB

The example above shows the categories recommended for the Open Strategy. They include the stock's Symbol, Last (price), Net Change, Bid (price), Ask (price), ATR (Average True Range), and HTB/ETB (Hard To Borrow or Easy To Borrow). These settings give the trader all they should need to quickly choose 3 stocks. Set their ATR high and low to determine their ATR revenue range, profit levels and the day's breakout range for trading one of the Open Strategies.

CHAPTER 5

6 Essential Studies and Indicators Used on Your Charts for Scalping the Open

5 Essential Studies Used on Your Charts for Scalping

Before diving into the specific open strategies that this book outlines, it is crucial for traders to have a firm grasp of several foundational technical analysis concepts. This chapter will cover the essential studies and indicators that traders must understand and effectively utilize to identify the potential entry and exit points of their trades. These include market volatility levels, oscillators, volume histograms, moving averages, support and resistance levels and more. Mastery of these elements will equip traders with the analytical skills necessary to successfully trade the open strategies.

1. Market Volatility
- ATR (Average True Range)

2. Oscillators
- RSI (Relative Strength Index)
- MACD (Moving Average Convergence Divergence)

3. Volume Histograms
- Volume Profile
- Standard Volume
- Custom Volume

4. Moving Averages
- SMA/EMA (Simple & Exponential Moving Averages)
- VWAP (Volume Weighted Average Price)

5. Fibonacci Retracement

6. Support and Resistance Levels

Average True Range (ATR)

The Average True Range (ATR) is a technical indicator commonly used by stock traders to measure the volatility and range of price movements of a stock. It provides insights into a stock's potential price range and its possible fluctuation during a given period.

The ATR quantifies the volatility of a stock by measuring the average range between the stock's high and low prices over a specified period. A higher ATR value suggests greater volatility, indicating larger price swings and potential trading opportunities. A lower ATR value suggests lower volatility and potentially less trading activity.

Traders often use the ATR to determine appropriate stop-loss levels. By multiplying the ATR by a predefined factor (e.g. 2 or 3), traders can establish a stop loss level that is proportional to the stock's volatility. This technique helps protect against excessive losses if the stock's price moves against the trader's position.

The ATR can also assist traders in determining the appropriate position size for a trade. By considering the ATR, traders can adjust their position size based on the volatility of the stock. For example, a higher ATR may warrant a smaller position size to manage risk, while a lower ATR may allow for a larger position size and can help traders identify potential breakout levels by determining if the current volatility exceeds historical volatility. Higher ATR values indicate increased potential for breakouts, while lower ATR values suggest limited price movement and potential range-bound trading.

Traders may employ volatility based trading strategies using the ATR. For example, they might initiate trades when the stock's price exceeds a certain multiple of the ATR, indicating increased volatility and potential trading opportunities.

Traders can also compare the ATR values of different stocks to identify those with higher or lower volatility. This information can be useful when selecting stocks for trading based on personal risk tolerance and trading strategies.

Because the price of securities can vary widely, the ATR may not always signify high volatility when selecting stocks for the Open Strategies #1 and #2. This is why using the volatility range formula and rating can be key to finding the right stocks to trade.

Example of Average True Range (ATR)

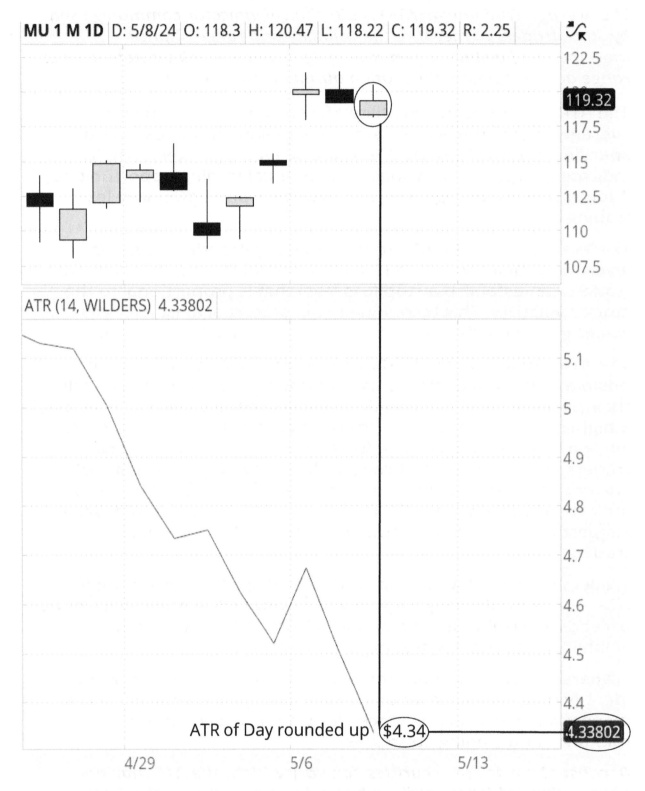

With the Open Strategy, the ATR is used to identify the upper and lower profit taking range, above or below the predetermined breakout range.

1. Oscillators

Oscillators are indicators that fluctuate above and below a fixed line or between set levels. They are typically used to identify overbought or oversold conditions. Common oscillators used for scalping the Open strategies include the RSI (Relative Strenth Index), and the MACD (Moving Average Convergence Divergence)

RSI (Relative Strength Index)

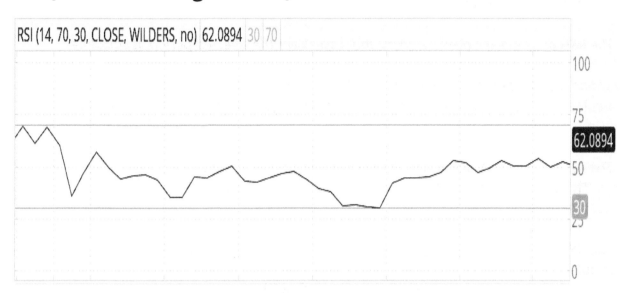

MACD (Moving Average Convergence Divergence)

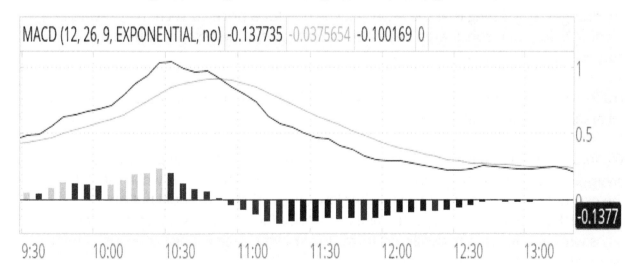

A deeper understanding of these two oscillators and a guideline of what to look for and how to use them before you begin trading an open strategy is explained in the following pages.

Relative Strength Index (RSI)

Relative Strength Index (RSI) is a popular technical indicator used in financial markets to assess the strength and momentum of price movements. It helps traders identify potential overbought or oversold conditions in an asset, which can signal a potential reversal or correction in price.

• *The RSI calculation requires selecting a specific time period, typically 14 periods of the time frame being used.* This can be adjusted based on the trader's preference and the characteristics of the asset being analyzed.

• *The RSI compares the average gains and losses over the selected period. It calculates the average gain by summing up the positive price changes over the period and dividing that sum by the number of periods.* Similarly, the average loss is calculated by summing up the negative price changes and dividing by the number of periods.

• *The Relative Strength (RS) is calculated by dividing the average gain by the average loss.* This provides a ratio of the average positive price changes to the average negative price changes.

• *The RSI value is derived using the relative strength. It is calculated using the formula:*

$$RSI = 100 - [100 / (1+ RS)]$$

• *The RSI value ranges from O to 100.* Typically a reading above 70 is considered overbought, suggesting that the asset may be due for a price correction or reversal. A reading below 30 is considered oversold, indicating that the asset may be due for a potential price bounce or recovery.

Traders may look for a RSI reading above 70 or below 30 to identify potential points of reversal or correction in the price of an asset.

Traders analyze the RSI in relation to the price action to identify divergences. Bullish divergence occurs when the price (or the candles) forms lower lows while the RSI (or the oscillator's average line) forms higher lows, indicating a potential bullish reversal. Bearish divergence occurs when the price (or the candles) forms higher highs while the RSI (or the oscillator) forms lower highs, suggesting potential bearish reversal.

Traders may also use the RSI to confirm the strength of a trend. In a strong uptrend the RSI tends to stay above 50, while in strong downtrends the RSI tends to stay below 50.

Example of Relative Strength Index (RSI)

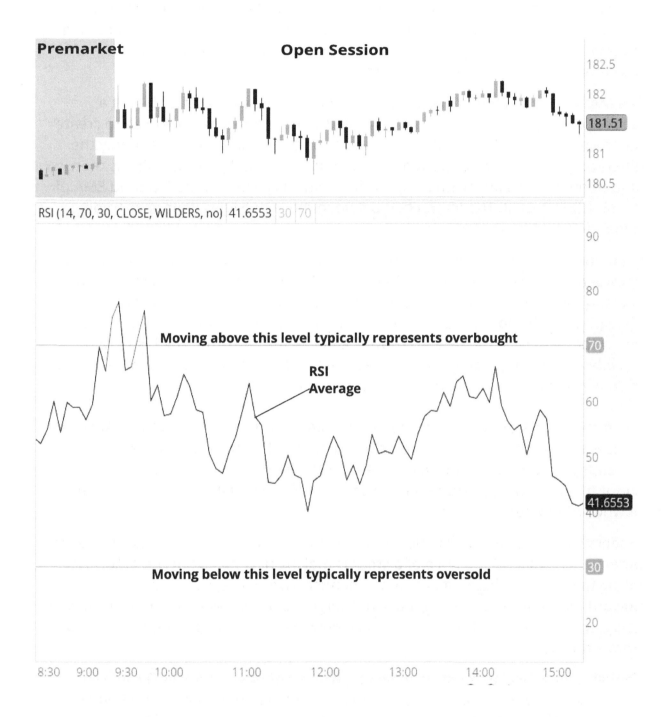

The Open Strategy uses the RSI for indications of a trend primarily during the open session 5 or 15 minute breakout time frames. If the RSI moves above or below the 50 level, it can be an indication of a trend. As the RSI moves steadily up to the 70 level or down to the 30 level it may indicate an imminent reversal. If these levels are about to be broken while in a position it can help traders decide whether to stay in the current trade.

Moving Average Convergence Divergence (MACD)

The Moving Average Convergence Divergence (MACD) is a powerful technical analysis tool used by traders to gauge momentum, trend direction, and potential reversals. It is particularly popular because it combines elements of both trend-following and momentum indicators.

The MACD is calculated using two exponential moving averages (EMAs) of a stock's price, typically over 12 and 26 periods. These two EMAs are used to create the main line of the MACD, often referred to as the "MACD line." It is simply the difference between the 12-period EMA and the 26-period EMA. This line is then plotted on a chart along with a "signal line," which is typically the 9-period EMA of the MACD line itself. The interaction between these two lines generates trading signals for market participants.

In addition to the MACD line and the signal line, the MACD chart will often include a histogram, which is a bar chart that shows the difference between the MACD line and the signal line. When the MACD line crosses above the signal line the histogram will be above the zero line, conversely when the MACD line crosses below the signal line the histogram will be below the zero line. The histogram provides a visual representation of the speed and direction of a price movement, making it easier for traders to identify changes in trend.

A common strategy is to enter a trade on a MACD crossover. When the MACD line crosses above the signal line, traders might enter a buy trade as it indicates increasing upward momentum or when the MACD line crosses below the signal line, it might be an opportune time to sell or short sell, as it indicates increasing downward momentum.

Traders look for divergence between the MACD and the price action as a signal of potential reversals. If the price of a stock is making new highs but the MACD is failing to reach new highs, it is a sign of bearish divergence, suggesting the upward momentum is waining. Bullish divergence occurs when the price is making new lows but the MACD is failing to make new lows, indicating potential reversal from a downtrend.

Though primarily a momentum indicator, when extended, the MACD can also reflect overbought or oversold conditions. Extended periods where the MACD is far above or below its signal line may indicate a pullback or reversal is imminent.

Example of
Moving Average Convergence Divergence (MACD)

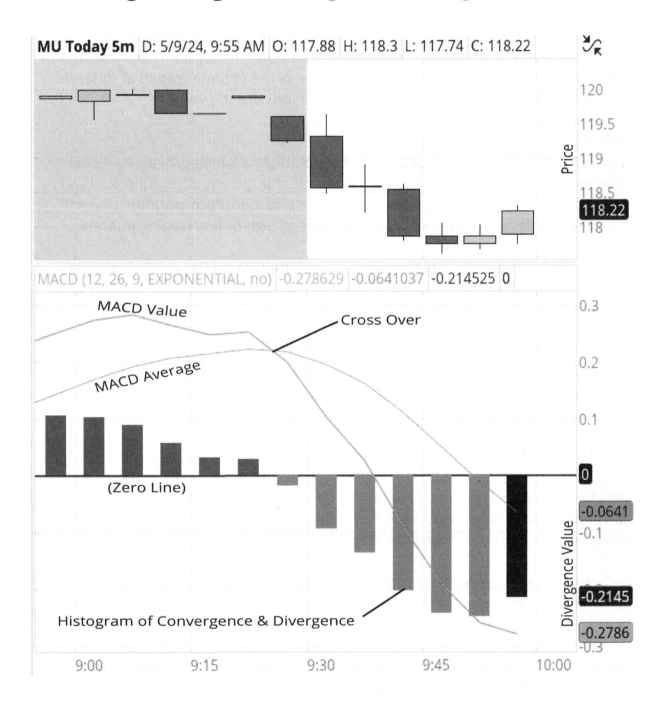

The Open Strategy uses the MACD for indications of a trend primarily during the open session 5 or 15 minute breakout time frames. If the MACD Value level crosses the average level it can be an indication of a trend reversal. The histogram level helps indicate this pending crossover by its proximity to the zero line giving the trader ample opportunity to recognize the pending reversal while in a position.

2. Volume Histograms

Volume histograms visually represent the trading volume in a market and can be either vertical or horizontal. Vertical volume histograms, typically placed below the price chart, show the volume traded durning specific time periods with bars that vary in height based on the volume. Horizontal volume histograms, like the Volume Profile, are placed along the price axis and display the volume traded at different price levels, with bars extending horizontaily to indicate the volume.

Volume Profile

Volume Profile is a feature available on most platforms which provides a visual representation of trading activity and volume distribution at different price levels over a specified period. It helps traders analyze and identify important support and resistance levels, as well as potential areas of high or low trading interest.

• The Volume Profile (VP) display is typically a histogram on the price chart. The horizontal bars represent the volume traded at each price level. The longer the bar, the higher the trading volume at that particular price level.

• Point of Control (POC), represents the price level with the highest traded volume within the selected period. It is often displayed as a line on the highlighted area of the Volume Profile. The POC can be a significant level of interest as it indicates the price level at which most trading activity occurred.

• The Value Area is a range of prices within the Volume Profile that contains a specified percentage of the total volume. Typically, a default is set to represent 70% of the volume. The Value area is often marked with lines or shaded regions on the Volume Profile. This helps identify the range of prices where most of the trading activity occurred during the selected period.

Traders can identify potential support and resistance levels using the Volume Profile. Areas with high trading volume, such as the POC and the Value Area may act as support or resistance, when the price approaches or interacts with them.

Traders can customize the time frame for the Volume Profile to analyze trading activity for different periods, such as intraday, daily, weekly or longer time periods. This allows traders to gain insights into volume distribution and market dynamics at various scales.

Example of Volume Profile (VP) on a 1-Minute Chart

MU Today 1m D: 5/9/24, 9:59 AM O: 118.14 H: 118.3 L: 118.11 C: 118.22 ...

This example shows the VP on a single day **"Today"**. You can see the high and low values in the center of the example bordering the darkened Value Area and the POC in the center. The VP set for intraday is very helpful. It shows the most current price action and can help predict entry and exit points. The VP study, used on the 1-min chart in this way, is commonly used by professional scalpers trading the Open Strategy to determine recent volume and price movement. Often, the horizontal bars moving across the chart, above or below the POC can signal the direction of the future short term price movement of the stock. This information can provide an extra edge for speedy trading decisions. *Remember, you must set the chart for **"Today 1m"** (not 1 day 1m) to affectively use the VP for intraday.*

Standard Volume Indicator on 1-Day 1-Minute Chart

This chart shows the candlesticks on a one-minute chart with the typical volume histogram below aligning with the candlesticks. The height of the volume bars indicate the strength of the volume for that particular candlestick time increment. On your chart, you will see the volume bars moving up and down in real-time, reflecting the current volume movement. Here, the grey bar indicates more buyers than sellers, the black bar shows there are more sellers than buyers, and the darker grey bar shows indecision. Many traders use this basic volume histogram when trading the Open Strategies as an additional tool on their platform to determine their entries and exits.

Example of Standard Volume Indicator

Professional Custom Volume Indicator

The Scalping Indicator is used by many professionals and is an extremely effective tool. This indicator shows the volume of the last candle and the current candle along with the percentages of buyers and sellers on the candlestick histogram in real-time.

Orginally designed for the **RV Strategy (DAY TRADING VOL 1)**, many professional scalpers soon realized it was also extremely helpful in fast moving momentum trading as well as with the **Open Strategies.** The scalping indicator is now recognized as one of the most valuable tools for scalping.

Below, the black line with dots signifies the sellers' sentiment; the gray line with dots the buyers' sentiment; both calculated using the close, low, and high of the current candle. The tall light gray rectangles show the overall volume. Above the histogram bars, the black boxes show (from left to right) the current volume, last candle's volume, what price action volume is stronger in the current candle (buyers or sellers), using percentages the final two boxes show the conflicting sentiment of buyers and sellers volume. Watching this indicator in real-time gives traders an advantage in predicting future short-term moves in the stock price action. This Indicator, primarily used by professionals, can be found on the **Million-Dollar-Margin Club** YouTube channel. Without this, traders could use the standard volume indicator supplied on most charts.

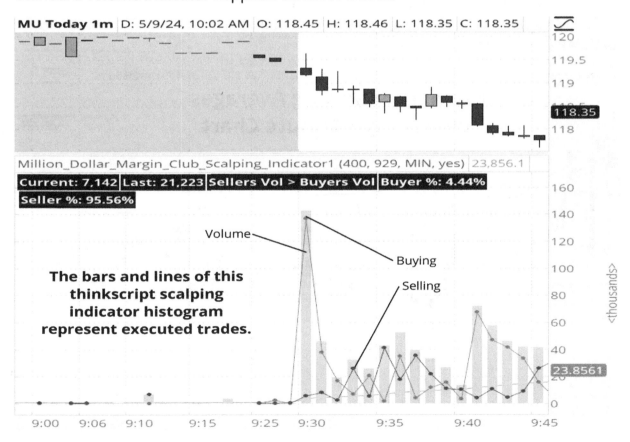

3. Moving Averages

Moving averages smooth out price data to create a single flowing line, making it easier to identify the direction of a trend.

Simple Moving Averages (SMA) give equal weighting to all values.
Exponential Moving Averages (EMA) give more weight to recent prices.
Volume-Weighted Average Price (VWAP) gives the average price a security has traded at throughout the day, based on both volume and price. It is a more comprehensive measure than an SMA, as it takes into account the volume of shares traded at different prices and is thus more reflective of the true market sentiment. Many short term traders use the **VWAP** to determine entries and exits of a trade as it is also considered emotional support or resistance when creating your profit levels for the Open Strategies. For more details about the SMA, EMA, or VWAP please refer to **DAY TRADING VOL 1.**

These tools are crucial for determining trend direction and potential reversal points for scalpers when using the Open Strategies.

① 20 SMA (Simple Moving Average for 20 bars)
② 50 SMA (Simple Moving Average for 50 bars)
③ 200 SMA (Simple Moving Average for 200 bars)
④ 9 EMA (Exponential Moving Average for 9 bars)
⑤ 20 EMA (Exponential Moving average for 20 bars)
⑥ VWAP (Volume Weighted Average Price)

Example of Moving Averages on a 2-Day 5-Minute Chart

4. Fibonacci Retracement

The Fibonacci Retracement is a popular technical analysis tool used by traders to identify potential levels of support and resistance when trading the Open Strategy . It is based on the Fibonacci sequence, a mathematical sequence where each number is the sum of the two preceding numbers (e.g., 0, 1, 1, 2, 3, 5, 8, 13, 21, etc.). The Fibonacci Retracement tool consists of horizontal lines drawn on a price chart at key Fibonacci ratios: 23.6%, 38.2%, 50%, 61.8%, 78.6%. These levels are calculated by measuring the distance between a significant high and low in a market and then applying the Fibonacci ratios to that range.

Traders use the Fibonacci Retracement tool to identify potential areas of price reversal or continuation. The theory being that markets tend to retrace a portion of a previous move before resuming the overall trend. The Fibonacci levels act as support or resistance zones, where traders are able to anticipate price reactions.

When using the Fibonacci Retracement Tool, traders typically start by identifying a significant high and low of a trend in a market or for a stock. The high represents a peak in price, while the low represents a decline. By drawing the Fibonacci Retracement tool left to right from the high to the low for a bullish retracement or the low to the high for a bearish retracement, the tool automatically plots the retracement levels on the chart.

Fibonacci Retracement levels can be combined with other technical analysis tools and indicators to strengthen trading decisions. Traders often look for confluences, where Fibonacci levels align with other support or resistance levels, trendlines, or key moving averages. These confluences increase the significance of the Fibonacci levels and provide more confidence in potential trade setups.

The chart below shows a typical Fibonacci retracement drawn for an Open Strategy. In this case the price action high (peak) on the left is marked along with the price action low (trough) on the right. The levels appear horizontally across the chart. As you can see from the candlesticks depicting the price action, the levels of the Fibonacci are often respected and the price action will often stop or reverse at these levels. This can help confirm a possible entry or exit of a trade. These levels are specifically used to help with the Open Strategies, but it is important to note other strategies may use this information differently. Some traders might enter and exit at specific Fibonacci ratios and not just any level.

Fibonacci ratios (23.6%, 38.2%, 61.8%, and sometimes 78.6% and 100%)which are derived from the **Fibonacci Sequence (1, 1, 2, 3, 5, 8, 13, 21, 34, 55 ...) also referred to as "nature's mathematical formula".**

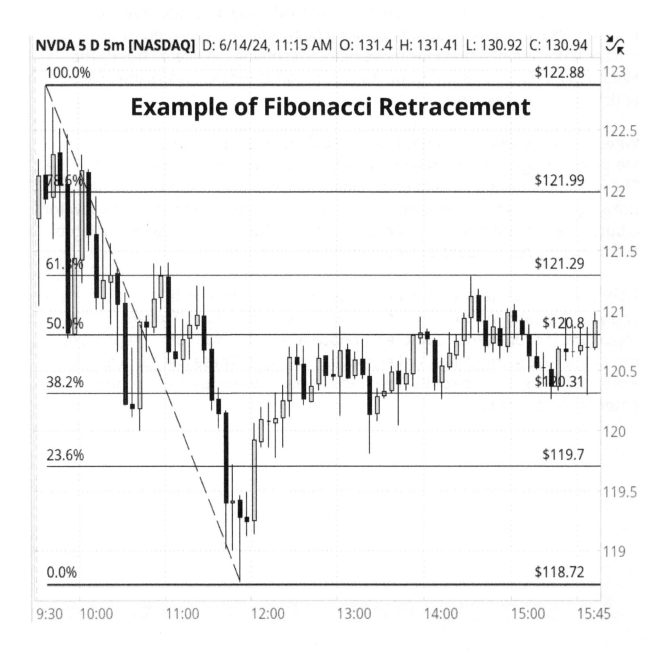

5. Support and Resistance Levels

Support and resistance levels are key concepts in technical analysis that help traders identify levels at which a stock's price tends to experience buying support or selling pressure respectively. These levels are drawn on a price chart to visually represent areas where the stock's price has historically reversed or stalled.

Support levels represent a price level at which the stock's price tends to find buying support, meaning that it is less likely to drop further. Traders believe that buyers (taking long positions) are more inclined to enter the market and purchase the stock when it reaches or nears the support level. The support level is typically drawn horizontally along the lowest point where the stock's price has bounced back or reversed direction in the past. Resistance levels represent a price level at which the stock's price encounters selling pressure, making it more difficult for the price to rise beyond the level. Traders believe that sellers (taking short positions) are more likely to enter the market and sell the stock when it reaches or nears a resistance level. The resistance line is usually drawn horizontally along the highest price points where the stocks price has reversed or encountered selling pressure in the past.

When a support level is breached, it suggests a potential shift in the stock sentiment, and a continuation of a downward move. If the price action was to go back up, the previous support level may now act as a resistance level and a barrier for future price increases. When a resistance level is breached, it suggests a potential shift in the stock sentiment, and a continuation of an upward move. If the price action was to go back down, the previous resistance level may now act as a support level and a barrier for future price decreases.

When identifying support and resistance levels, traders often consider trading volume. Higher trading volume near a support or resistance level can provide additional confirmation of its significance. High volume during a breakout or breakdown of a support or resistance level may indicate increased buying or selling interest respectively.

CHAPTER 6

Learning the Rules and Applying Your Tools, Studies, and Indicators to Effectively Trade the Open Strategies

The Open Strategies are designed to capitalize on short-term price trends at the market open.

The 4 different strategies in this book offer multiple opportunities to identify and profit from potential breakouts.

Each strategy is based on a different time frame. Depending on your trading plan any of these strategies can work for you. Each could have a better than 60% chance of success based on thousands of hours of back testing.

Once you decide on the Open Strategy you're going to trade, it is extremely important to follow the trading rules and guidelines of the strategy to assure a higher probability of success. The following pages will show you how to find the best stocks to trade, calculate an ATR revenue range and the Volatility Rating, mark out your breakout range and profit/pivot levels, provide guidelines and rules for trading the 4 Open Strategies, and how to utilize indicators such as standard volume, volume profile, custom volume histogram, VWAP, Moving Averages, and MACD when trading these strategies.

Have a Detailed Understanding of the 4 Open Strategies and Their Rules to Achieve Success

Open Strategy #1 and #2 Breakout Ranges

Open Strategy #1 (7:30 to 9:15 Premarket Breakout Range) looks at the price range and timeframe when the premarket volume begins to increase as more traders start their trading day. From market open, suggested trading time is 15 minutes.

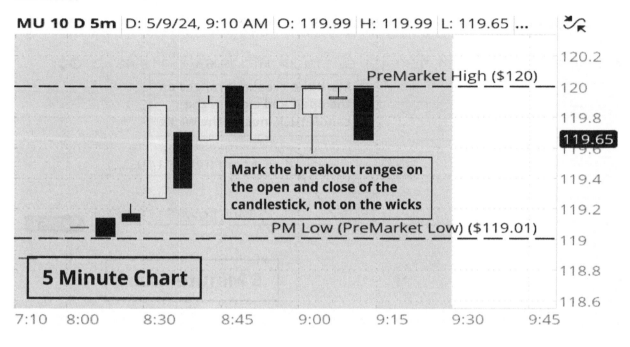

Open Stratgey #2 (8:30 to 9:00 Premarket Breakout Range) looks at the last full 30-minute candle of the premarket, this takes an average of more recent price. From market open, suggested trading time is 30 minutes.

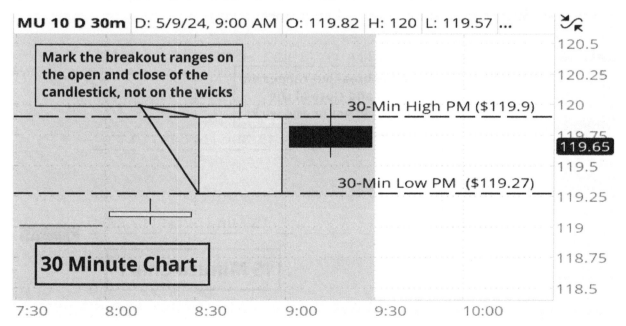

Open Strategy #3 and #4 Breakout Ranges

Open Strategy #3 (9:30 to 9:35 Open Market Session Breakout Range) looks at the first five minutes of the open session, when price action can be far more volatile than during premarket and may provide a more accurate price level for a potential breakout into a trend. The close of the candle may call for an immediate entry. Suggested trading time is 30 minutes.

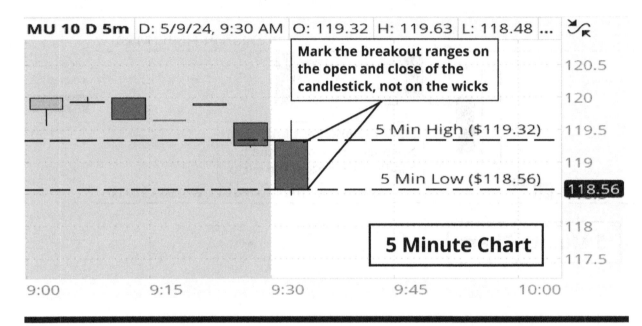

Open Strategy #4 (9:30 to 9:45 Open Market Breakout Range) looks at the first fifteen minute candle of the open session to close before entering a trade. This is considered by many to be the most accurate forecast of an upcoming trend as it breaks. Suggested trading time is 45 minutes.

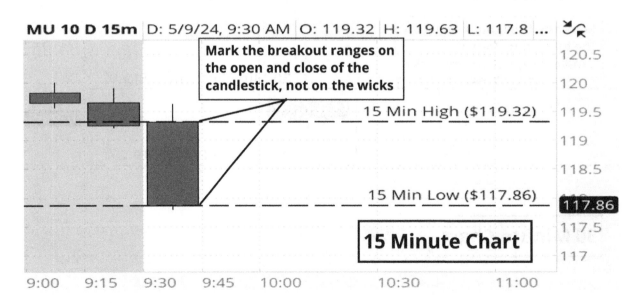

Step 1:
Scanner Criteria and Specifications
to Find Stocks for the Open Strategies

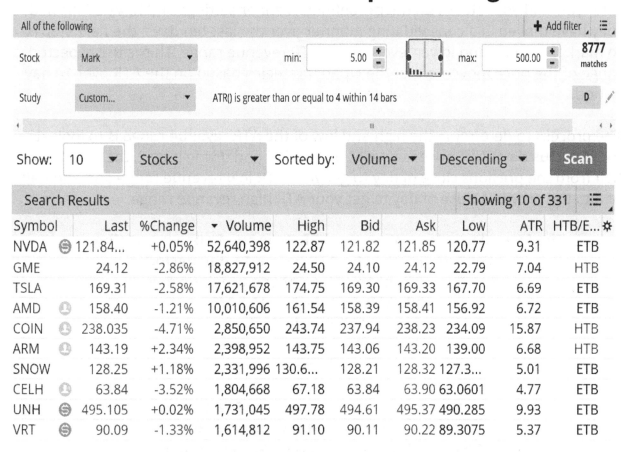

Symbol		Last	%Change	▼ Volume	High	Bid	Ask	Low	ATR	HTB/E...⚙
NVDA	Ⓢ	121.84...	+0.05%	52,640,398	122.87	121.82	121.85	120.77	9.31	ETB
GME		24.12	-2.86%	18,827,912	24.50	24.10	24.12	22.79	7.04	HTB
TSLA		169.31	-2.58%	17,621,678	174.75	169.30	169.33	167.70	6.69	ETB
AMD	◕	158.40	-1.21%	10,010,606	161.54	158.39	158.41	156.92	6.72	ETB
COIN	◕	238.035	-4.71%	2,850,650	243.74	237.94	238.23	234.09	15.87	HTB
ARM	◕	143.19	+2.34%	2,398,952	143.75	143.06	143.20	139.00	6.68	HTB
SNOW		128.25	+1.18%	2,331,996	130.6...	128.21	128.32	127.3...	5.01	ETB
CELH	◕	63.84	-3.52%	1,804,668	67.18	63.84	63.90	63.0601	4.77	ETB
UNH	Ⓢ	495.105	+0.02%	1,731,045	497.78	494.61	495.37	490.285	9.93	ETB
VRT	Ⓢ	90.09	-1.33%	1,614,812	91.10	90.11	90.22	89.3075	5.37	ETB

Set your scanner specifications for a custom ATR study within 14 bars (14-day period) equal to $4 or greater and the Mark (stock) with a minimum and maximum price range between $5 and $500. Set the Show for 10 (stocks), sort by volume, set for descending, and then press Scan. Always verify that the stock is easy to borrow (ETB), so you can take your trades either long and short. Look at the highest volume stocks first to see if they meet the criteria.

After you have found 3 stocks under search results, look on your daily chart over a 10 day period and make sure the price action has been fairly consolidated to give you the best chance for a short term breakout. When implementing any of the four Open Strategies you should look for a consolidating pre-market pattern where the price action has not moved more than half the value of its ATR up or down. This is important to monitor prior to the open in case of a huge price swing.

If you are trading Open Strategy #1 or Open Strategy #2, you should also look for a stock with a volatility rating around 25% or lower. The lower the volatility rating the more likely the price action will move through the breakout range.

Step 2:
How to Mark The ATR Revenue Range

After you find your stocks on the predefined scanner settings and have confirmed they have moved in a consolidating manner over the last ten days, the next step is to mark the upper and lower levels of the ATR revenue range. This is the expected range of the price movement of the Open Strategies based on the ATR over 14 day period.

The process to determine the high and low of the ATR revenue range is to look at the previous day's ATR price over a 14 day period and divide it by 2, then subtract half from the previous close of day to get your ATR low revenue range and add half of it to the previous close of day to get your ATR high revenue range.

The formula to determine the ATR Revenue Range is as follows:
Let A represent the ATR over a 14-day period
Let C represent the close of the previous day.
Half ATR Calculation: H = A/2
Lower ATR Range: L= C - H
Upper ATR Range: U = C + H
Where
H is half of the ATR
L is the Lower ATR Range or ATR Low
U is the Upper ATR Range or ATR High
The ATR Revenue Range is represented as
ATR Revenue Range = (L, U)

ATR Revenue Range Graphic

The determination of the ATR high and ATR low levels on this chart are as follows:
ATR High = previous day close + ATR/2 for example: $121.48 = $119.32 + ($4.33/2)
ATR Low = previous day close - ATR/2 for example: $117.16 = 119.32 - ($4.33/2)

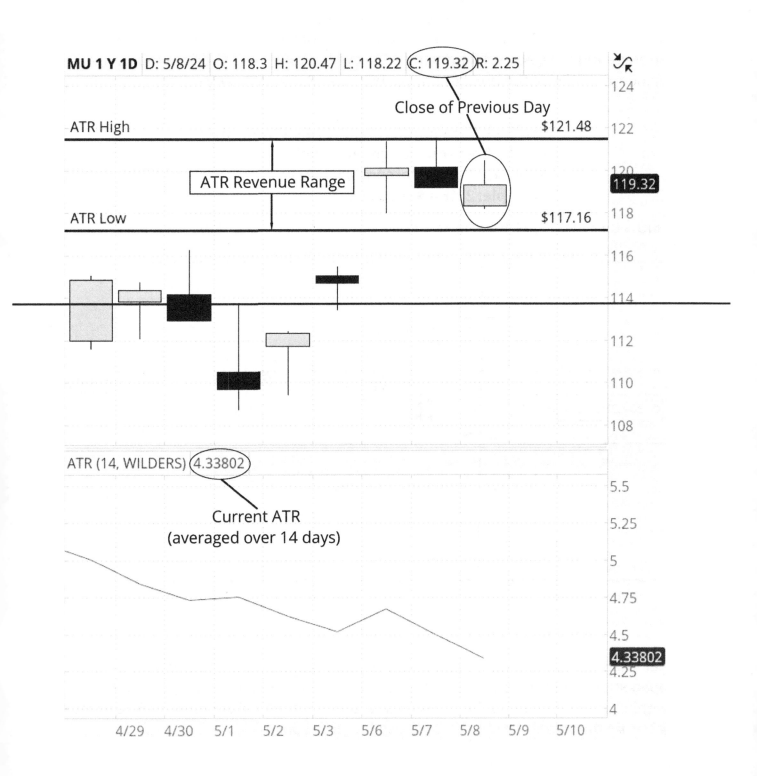

Step 3:
How to Measure Your Volatility Rating for Open Strategies #1 and #2

You should try to find a stock to trade with a volatility rating of 25% or less, if possible, to assure a better chance of a price action breakout signaling a short-term trend. To find your stocks volatility rating percentage for the open strategy you are trading, identify the ATR revenue range and the Breakout range values, then divide the breakout range by the ATR revenue range.

Let R = ATR revenue range (typical volatility)
Let B = breakout range (early volatility)
Volatility Rating Percentage = B/R
Example: 22% = $.99/$4.32

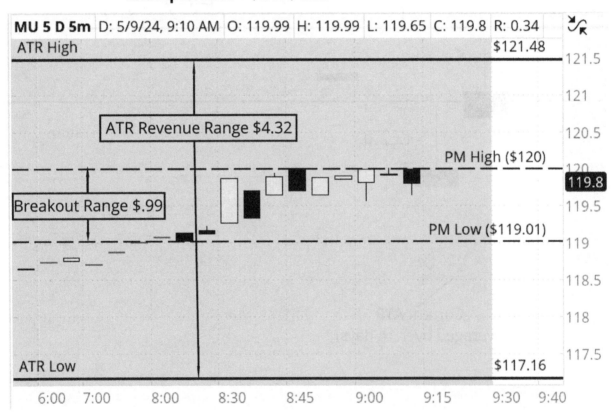

Below 25% is considered an acceptable ratio for a probability of a breakout of the open strategies' pre-defined range and offers a much better chance for trading within the open strategies' time parameters. If you are trading the Open Strategies #3 or #4 the volatility rating is rarely used to time constraints.

Step 4:

Mark the 10-Day Fibonacci Retracements

This chart shows the Fibonacci retracement levels marked for the Open Strategy on a 10-day 5-Minute chart. Always mark the high or low from left to right. This identifies the first of the profit levels.

Fibonacci Retracement on a 10-Day 5-Minute Chart

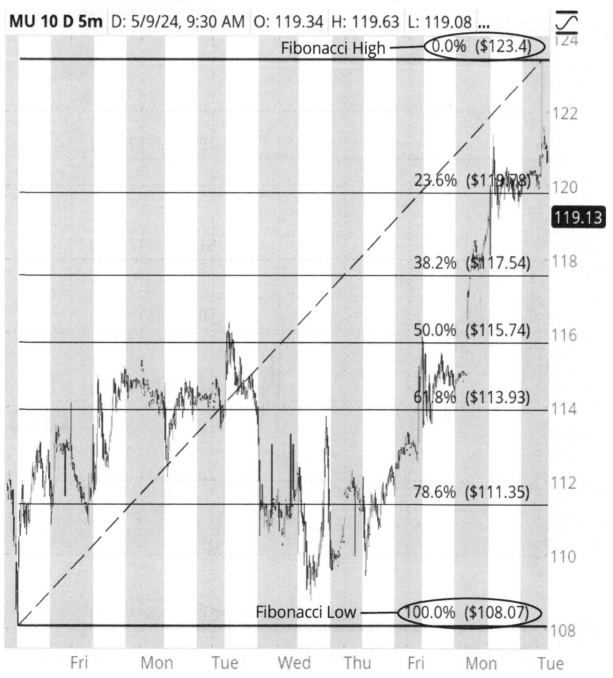

Step 5:
Mark the 2-Day Fibonacci Retracements

This chart shows the Fibonacci retracement levels marked for the Open Strategy on a 2 day 5 Minute chart. Always mark the high or low from left to right.

Fibonacci Retracement on a 2 Day 5-Minute Chart

Step 6:
Mark your Profit/Pivot levels between your ATR Revenue Range

Profit Level lines are marked on a candle's body or wick when identified as a pivot point in the price action. These profit/pivot levels are further confirmed when other candles' bodies or wicks also start or end at the same price level. The ATR revenue range high and low represent limits of the price range to mark profit/pivot levels. Once you mark the breakout range of the Open Strategy you're trading, remove any profit/pivot levels that are within the breakout range high and low. No trades should be taken between the high or low breakout range levels. The profit levels above the premarket high, as shown in the example, become signals for entering and exiting trades for long positions.

Example of Profit/Pivot Levels Above Breakout Range

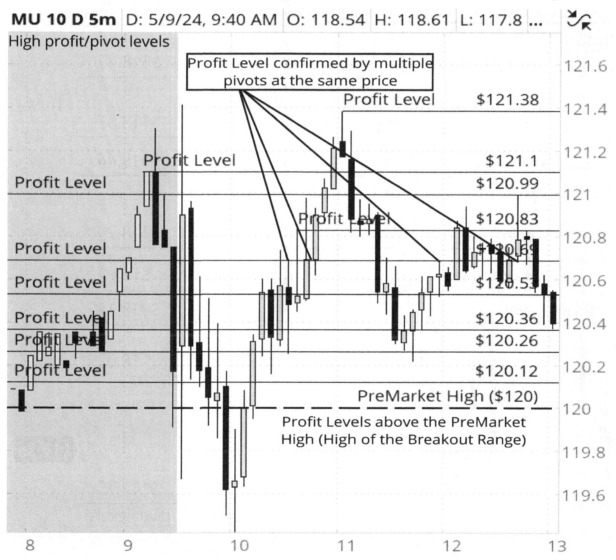

The Profit (profit/pivot) Levels are marked on a 5-minute chart that is set for a 10-day interval. Any 5-minute candle that reverses the previous candle's direction can be a profit/pivot point. Confirmation of these profit/pivot points comes when other 5-minute candles start or end at the same price at either the body or wick. The Profit (profit/pivot) Levels below the PreMarket Low, as shown in the example below, become signals for entering and exiting trades for short positions.

Example of Profit/Pivot Levels Below Breakout Range

MU 10 D 5m   D: 5/9/24, 9:40 AM   O: 118.54   H: 118.61   L: 117.8 ...

PM Low (PreMarket Low) $119.01
                                                            119

Profit Levels below the PreMarket
Low (Low of the Breakout Range)

Profit Level $118.82
Profit Level $118.76   118.8

Profit Level confirmed by multiple
pivots at the same price   Profit Level $118.65

                                                            118.6
                        Profit Level $118.52
Profit Level $118.44
                                                            118.4
Profit Level $118.29
Profit Level $118.2
                                                            118.2
Profit Level $118.13

                        Profit Level $118.02
                                                            118

                                                            117.86
Profit Level $117.75   117.8
                                                            Low profit/pivot levels

5   6   7   8   9   10   11   12

The example below shows the premarket 7:30-9:15 EST breakout strategy for Open Strategy #1 and how the price moved during the first 15 minutes of trading. The Profit (profit/pivot) Levels between the ATR revenue range consist of the 10-day Fibonacci retracements, 2-day Fibonacci retracements, and the 5-minute profit/pivot levels based on historical data from the last 10 days.

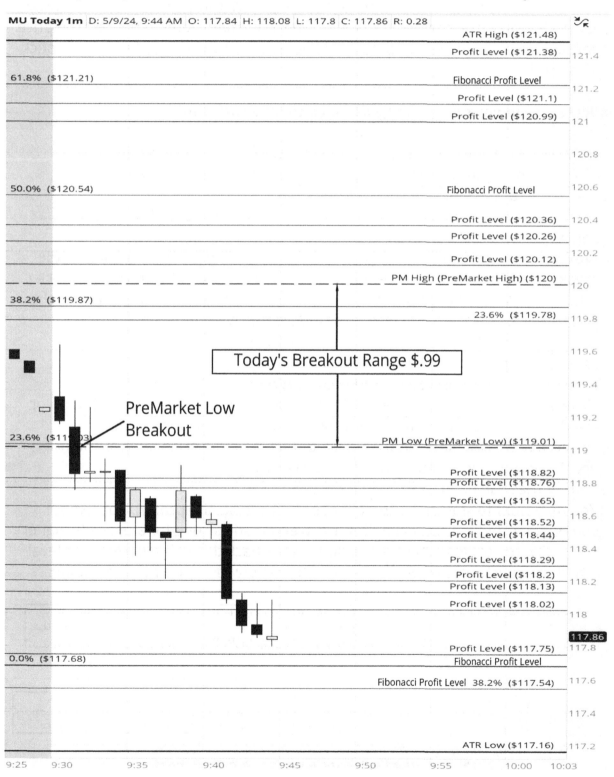

Rules and Guidelines When Trading Open Strategies

The Open Strategies are short-term breakout strategies. The 4 different strategies have specific time parameters to identify their breakout ranges and are always traded using a 1-minute candlestick chart. Often traders will immediately take their first trade on Open Strategies #3 and #4 as they mark the 5-minute or 15- minute breakout levels on the candlestick bodies. This is primarily due to the fact the price action will have already reached the breakout range at the close of the candlestick just marked.

Follow these important trading guidelines to take your trades.

1. Only take a trade when the price action passes the breakout range as either a long or short position depending on the direction of the breakout.
2. Take profit at the first profit/pivot level.
3. Only trade long positions above the high breakout level and short positions below the low breakout level.
4. After you take profit at a profit/pivot level, wait until the next 1-minute candle breaks through a profit/pivot level before you enter your next trade. The price action must be past the open of this 1-minute candle in the same direction the price action is trending. * *(If your chart indicates upward moving candles are green and downward moving candles are red, you should only take a trade long as you break a pivot/profit level if the candle is green and only take a trade short as you break a pivot/profit level if the candle is red)*
5. Have a trading plan that has a maximum loss per trade to exit your position or exit if the price action retraces halfway through the previous candle.
6. Never take a trade between the breakout high and low price range or before the first 1-minute candle of the open session closes.
7. Your entries can be market or limit orders.
8. You may want to stay in the trend longer as it breaks the profit/pivot levels if your studies and indicators confirm the trend is still strong for a possible higher profit. Exit the trade as the price action breaks back through a profit/pivot level it had previously passed or if your indicators show the trend may be ending.

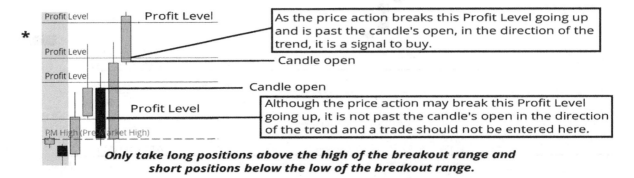

Only take long positions above the high of the breakout range and short positions below the low of the breakout range.

After you enter a trade, continuous assessment is crucial for success. As detailed in the "Open Strategy" you are equipped with multiple entry strategies based on premarket and early session price movement breakouts.

The essence of this approach lies in identifying price action after the first initial breakout and then managing the trade by interpreting various technical indicators and studies. This information can help you decide whether to hold your position at the profit/pivot levels for a continuation of the move or exit the trade to secure gains. Once you have entered a position based on a breakout level (using one of the predefined ranges of the open strategies) you should closely monitor all the studies and indicators on your platform to help with verification to determine whether to exit the trade at the first profit/pivot level, remain in the trade as it moves toward the next profit/pivot level, or exit a losing trade based on your trading plan or if the price action retraces half of the previous 1-minute candle.

Utilize the following studies to help determine your entries and exits at profit/pivot levels

The Standard Volume Histogram is the most often used indicator to determine entry and exit levels while using the open strategies. Assessing volume patterns with your volume histograms are invaluable as they provide insights into the strength behind a price move. An increase in volume along with a price move in the desired direction may suggest stong buyer or seller verification, validating the continuation of the trade. Diminishing volume may signal a lack of conviction among traders, prompting consideration of an exit.

The Volume Profile study as customized in chapter 5, is a volume histogram that tracks the amount of volume at each price level in a certain time frame as the stock moves. This histogram shows you where price levels have historically had a high or low amount of trading volume. When you set your Volume Profile study for Intraday on your chart, you can see more clearly where the most recent premarket and early open session price action had the highest volume. Take note of the Point Of Control, Value High, and Value Low levels within the Volume Profile study and how they relate to your pivot/profit levels. If the Volume Profile levels show recent higher or lower volume at these pivot/price levels it can give you verification of a potential continuation or reversal. Identifying these levels before you enter your trade, and watching the price action as it nears them, can act as additional guidance to help manage the trade. When the price action reaches these levels, watch the current 1-minute standard volume indicator as well to see if it is increasing or decreasing near the pivot/profit levels to further confirm your decision to remain in or exit the trade.

Custom indicators such as the **Million-Dollar-Margin Club's Scalping Indicator** replaces the standard volume indicator for most professionals and can be very helpful to traders as they trade the fast moving price action at the open. This custom indicator available on the "Million-Dollar-Margin Club" YouTube channel, shows the buyers and sellers within the volume bar and the percentage of each in real time. Watching this indicator which has multiple tiers of information can help you with rapid decision making giving you a jump on a fast momentum directional move.

VWAP (Volume Weighted Average Price)
While trading the Open Strategies in the early market, the VWAP can help gauge the possible direction of the stock's future price action. If the price action is above the VWAP it may indicate an upward trend, and if the price action is below the VWAP it may indicate a downward trend. The location of the VWAP might help you decide how strong the price move is in its currents direction before you enter or exit a trade. Trading above the VWAP may indicate strong bullish sentiment, supporting a decision to enter or hold a long position. Trading below the VWAP may indicate a bearish sentiment, supporting a decision to take or hold a short position.

Moving Averages
Identifying the price of action (on either your 1-minute or 5-minute chart as shown on page 60) of the 9-EMA can provide you information on the strength of a short term price trend in its relationship to the 20-EMA. As the gap widens it can be a sign of a strong continuation of the current price action. As the upward or downward direction of both averages align or narrow, they indicate the direction of the current price action is getting weaker, and shows a possible signal of the trend ending. Often a crossover of the 9-EMA past the 20-EMA gives you a more certain sign of change in price movement direction. Before and after you enter a trade, it is important to watch these values so you can assess the strength of the ongoing price action.

MACD (Moving Average Divergence Convergence)
The MACD study can give further verification of changes in price action and can signal whether to enter, exit, or hold a trade using the open strategies. A buy signal is typically indicated when the MACD crosses above the signal line. This crossover suggests that the short-term momentum is stronger than the long-term momentum indicating an upward trend and is further confirmed by a greater divergence. A sell signal is given when the MACD crosses below the signal line. this indicates the short-term momentum is weakening compared to long-term momentum, suggesting a downward trend and is further confirmed by a greater divergence.

Summary for preparing to trade the Open Strategies

Make a trading plan that has a maximum loss per trade and loss per day.

Decide on the Open Strategy you're going to trade today. You can always change to a different strategy as the time moves closer or into the open session.

Find at least 3 stocks using the predefined scanner settings.

For the best results, determine on a daily chart that these stocks have moved in a consolidating pattern over a ten day period, meaning the open and close of the last daily candle intersects with the price action levels of as many of the previous 10-day candles bodies as possible. This will offer multiple profit/pivot point levels to identify for trading the Open Strategies. Then further look for a consolidating pre-market pattern that should be less than 1/2 the price action up or down of the previous day's ATR. This will provide the best possibility for a short-term breakout of all the Open Strategies as the market opens.

Enter your stocks on your watchlist daily guidelines in order of the best 10 day and premarket consolidations.

Mark the ATR revenue levels on your chart for the stock you're considering.

Set the 2 day and 10 day Fibonacci retracement levels.

Mark all your profit/pivot levels between the ATR revenue range.

For Open Strategies #1 and #2, you should determine the volatility rating as soon as possible to improve your stock selection, this should give you the best possibility for the stocks short-term breakout.

Mark the breakout range, high and low as per the Open Strategy you're trading (if you haven't already). If any of the profit/pivot levels fall between the high and low of the breakout range levels they should be removed.

Remember, only enter a trade after the price action moves through the breakout range. While watching your studies, indicators, and the overall volume of the stock, exit your trade at a profit/pivot level that meets your trading plan. Watch closely to make sure you don't exceed your maximum loss for each trade. A typical exit if the price action is going against your trade, is to exit as the price retraces halfway through the previous candle or reaches your maxiumum loss per trade as outlined in your trading plan.

Only trade within the time allowed for the open strategy you are trading.

CHAPTER 7

Trading Examples

Your Pathway to Success is Ahead

These Examples Provide a
Clear Pathway to Your Success

Find the open strategy that is best for you by trading in a simulator first or with a very low share size. Once your backtesting has proved the best open strategy for you, only then should you trade with real money or scale up to a higher share size.

With the following examples, profit can vary depending on your risk/reward day trading plan. The win percentage ranges between 61% to 66%, so if you have a one to one or better risk/reward ratio called for in your trading plan you would have profited. This rating has proven to be very consistent over time as backtested by professional traders. Remember to always follow your maximum loss per trade and for the day. Follow the Open Strategies' loss prevention protocol by exiting at the retracement of half of the previous candle.

The examples and descriptions of the 4 open strategies are based on finished candles which represent the open, close, high, and low of the price action as shown in **Figure 1.** It is possible the candlestick movements depicting the price action may have retraced multiple times before the stationary chart picture was captured in the examples of the marked entry and exits of each trade.

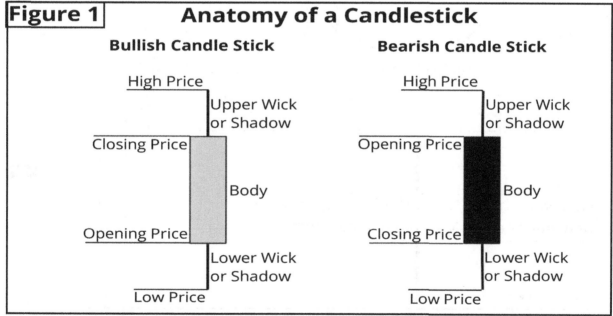

It's important to understand, only a single trade should be taken per 1-minute candle. The basic strategy is to enter the trade when the candle's price action passes the breakout range or a profit/pivot level based on the open strategy trading guidelines, and exit when the first profit/pivot level is reached. An alternative method is to let the price action continue as it breaks additional profit/pivot levels, and only exit for a profit when the price retraces half of the previous candle or back to the last level.

Open Strategy #1
(Pre-Market Breakout Range) 7:30 am to 9:15 am
Complete Layout Example

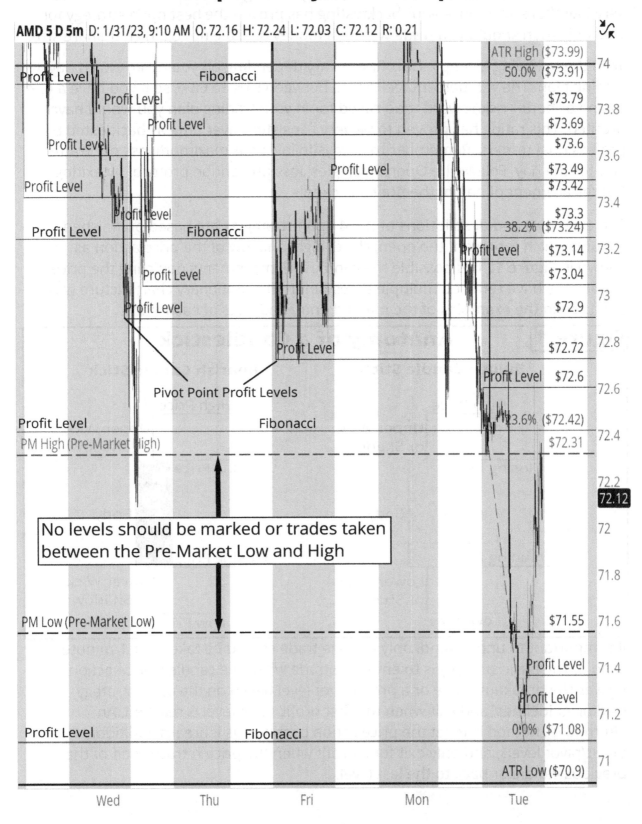

AMD 5 D 5m D: 1/31/23, 9:10 AM O: 72.16 H: 72.24 L: 72.03 C: 72.12 R: 0.21

ATR High ($73.99)

Profit Level · Fibonacci · 50.0% ($73.91) · 74

Profit Level · $73.79 · 73.8

Profit Level · $73.69

Profit Level · $73.6

Profit Level · $73.6

Profit Level · $73.49 · 73.6

Profit Level · $73.42

Profit Level · $73.4

Profit Level · $73.3

Profit Level · Fibonacci · 38.2% ($73.24)

Profit Level · $73.14 · 73.2

Profit Level · $73.04

Profit Level · $72.9 · 73

Profit Level · $72.72 · 72.8

Profit Level · $72.6 · 72.6

Pivot Point Profit Levels

Profit Level · Fibonacci · 23.6% ($72.42)

PM High (Pre-Market High) · $72.31 · 72.4

72.2

72.12

No levels should be marked or trades taken between the Pre-Market Low and High

72

71.8

PM Low (Pre-Market Low) · $71.55 · 71.6

Profit Level · 71.4

Profit Level · 71.2

Profit Level · Fibonacci · 0.0% ($71.08)

71

ATR Low ($70.9)

Wed   Thu   Fri   Mon   Tue

Open Strategy #1
(Pre-Market Breakout Range) Closeup Example

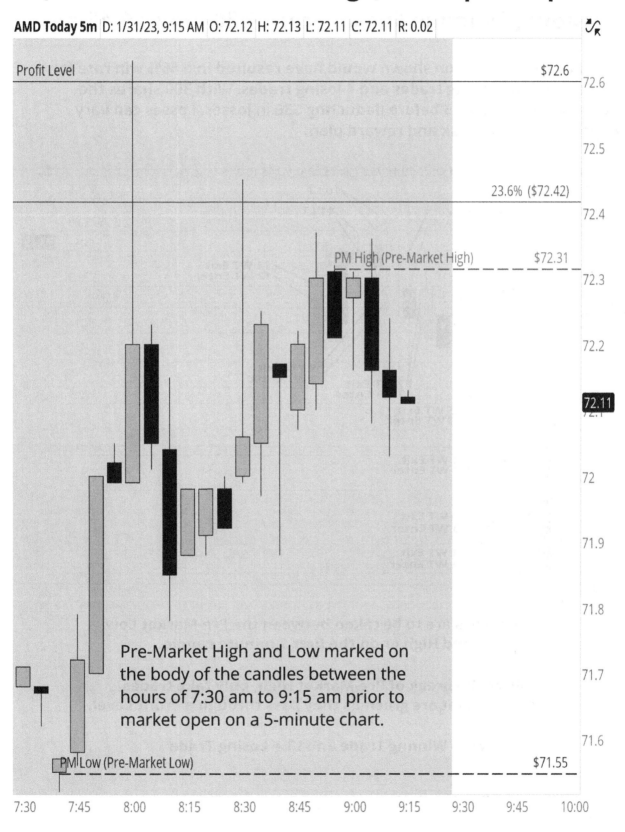

AMD Today 5m D: 1/31/23, 9:15 AM O: 72.12 H: 72.13 L: 72.11 C: 72.11 R: 0.02

Profit Level — $72.6

23.6% ($72.42)

PM High (Pre-Market High) — $72.31

72.11

Pre-Market High and Low marked on the body of the candles between the hours of 7:30 am to 9:15 am prior to market open on a 5-minute chart.

PM Low (Pre-Market Low) — $71.55

7:30   7:45   8:00   8:15   8:30   8:45   9:00   9:15   9:30   9:45   10:00

Open Strategy #1
(Pre-Market Breakout Range)
Trading Example Shows From 9:30 am to 9:45 am

Trading the price action shown would have resulted in a 66% win rate for trades, with 8 winning trades and 4 losing trades. With 300 shares the potential profit is $255 before deducting $36 in losses. Losses can vary depending on your risk and reward plan.

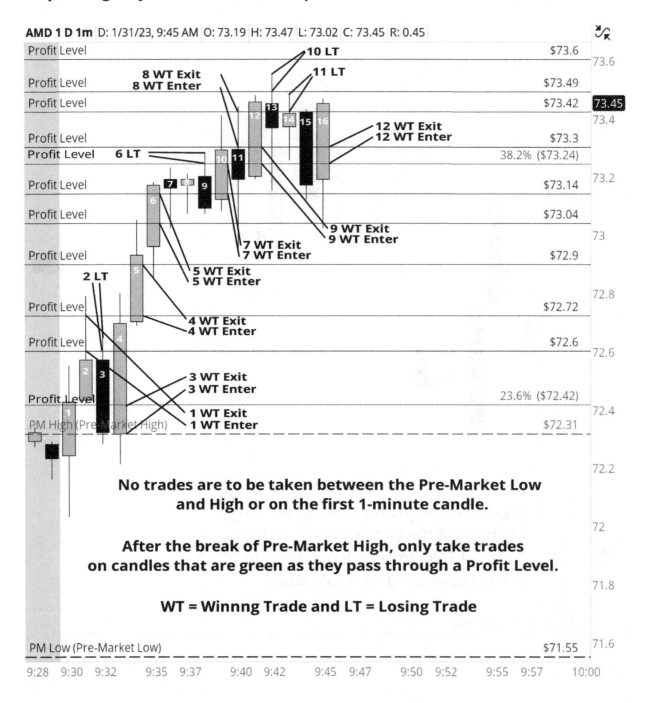

AMD 1 D 1m D: 1/31/23, 9:45 AM O: 73.19 H: 73.47 L: 73.02 C: 73.45 R: 0.45

No trades are to be taken between the Pre-Market Low and High or on the first 1-minute candle.

After the break of Pre-Market High, only take trades on candles that are green as they pass through a Profit Level.

WT = Winnng Trade and LT = Losing Trade

Trade Description for Open Strategy #1
For Examples Shown on Page 88

The trade descriptions below show the details of each trade seen in the trading examples. All trades were based on limit orders at the entry and exit of the profit/pivot levels. This assures more exact entries and exits and is important when trying to take profit at tight profit/pivot levels that might be as low as 5 cents.

1. Enter a position on candle 2 as it breaks the profit level at $72.60 and the first exit is at the profit level at $72.72
2. Losing Trade on candle 3
3. Enter a position on candle 4 as it breaks the Pre-Market High at $72.31 and the first exit is at the profit level at $72.42
4. Enter a position on candle 5 as it breaks the profit level at $72.72 and the first exit is at the profit level at $72.90
5. Enter a position on candle 6 as it breaks the profit level at $73.04 and the first exit is at the profit level at $73.14
6. Losing Trade on candle 9
7. Enter a position on candle 10 as it breaks the profit level at $73.14 and the first exit is at the profit level at $73.24
8. Enter a position on candle 11 as it breaks the profit level at $73.30 and the first exit is at the profit level at $73.42
9. Enter a position on candle 12 as it breaks the Fibonacci profit level at $73.24 and the first exit is at the profit level at $73.30
10. Losing Trade on candle 13
11. Losing Trade on candle 14
12. Enter a position on candle 16 as it breaks the Fibonacci profit level at $73.24 and the first exit is at the profit level at $73.30

A more aggressive method for taking profits would be to wait until the price action retraces to the last profit level it breaks through before you exit. The advantage to this is that you may extend your profits to the next level. The downside is the price may retrace too quickly through the level to capture the optimum profit. This method relies heavily on scalping experience but may lead to greater profits.

Open Strategy #2
(Pre-Market 30 Minute Breakout)
Complete Setup Example

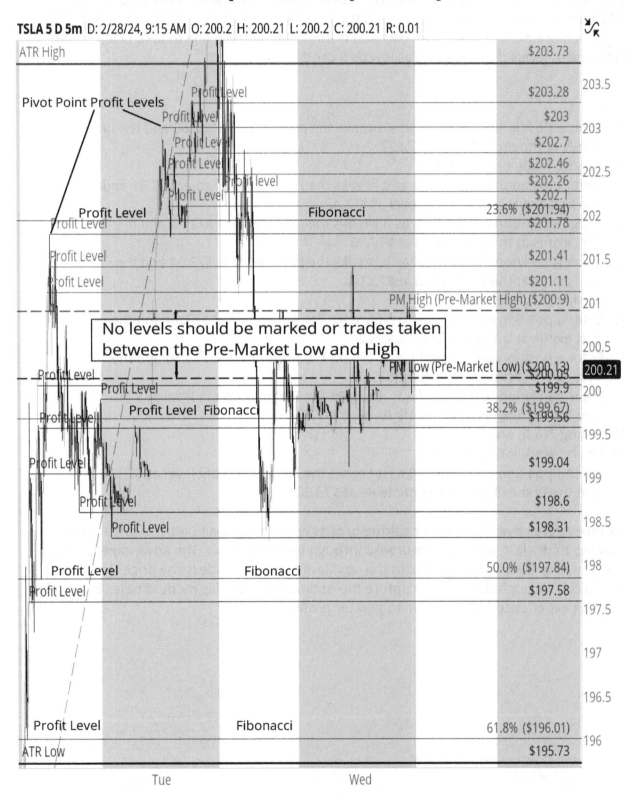

TSLA 5 D 5m D: 2/28/24, 9:15 AM O: 200.2 H: 200.21 L: 200.2 C: 200.21 R: 0.01

ATR High — $203.73

Pivot Point Profit Levels

Profit Level — $203.28 (203.5)

Profit Level — $203 (203)

Profit Level — $202.7

Profit Level — $202.46 (202.5)

Profit level — $202.26

Profit Level — $202.1

Profit Level — Fibonacci — 23.6% ($201.94) (202)

Profit Level — $201.78

Profit Level — $201.41 (201.5)

Profit Level — $201.11

PM High (Pre-Market High) ($200.9) (201)

No levels should be marked or trades taken between the Pre-Market Low and High

(200.5)

PM Low (Pre-Market Low) ($200.13)

Profit Level — $200.03

Profit Level — $199.9 (200)

Profit Level — Fibonacci — 38.2% ($199.67)

Profit Level — $199.56

(199.5)

Profit Level — $199.04 (199)

Profit Level — $198.6

Profit Level — $198.31 (198.5)

Profit Level — Fibonacci — 50.0% ($197.84) (198)

Profit Level — $197.58

(197.5)

(197)

(196.5)

Profit Level — Fibonacci — 61.8% ($196.01)

(196)

ATR Low — $195.73

Tue   Wed

Open Strategy #2
(Pre-Market 30 Minute Breakout) Closeup Example

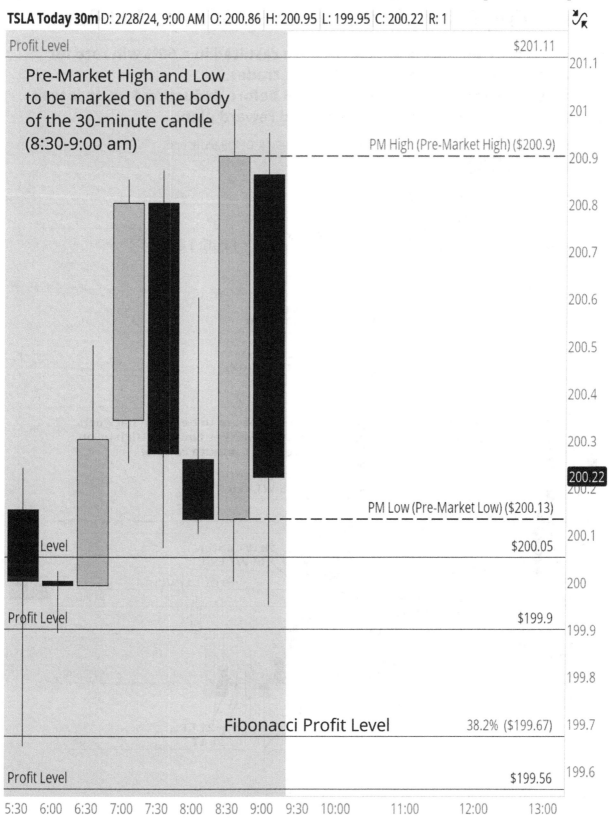

TSLA Today 30m D: 2/28/24, 9:00 AM O: 200.86 H: 200.95 L: 199.95 C: 200.22 R: 1

Profit Level — $201.11

Pre-Market High and Low to be marked on the body of the 30-minute candle (8:30-9:00 am)

PM High (Pre-Market High) ($200.9)

200.22

PM Low (Pre-Market Low) ($200.13)

Level — $200.05

Profit Level — $199.9

Fibonacci Profit Level — 38.2% ($199.67)

Profit Level — $199.56

5:30 6:00 6:30 7:00 7:30 8:00 8:30 9:00 9:30 10:00 11:00 12:00 13:00

Open Strategy #2
(30-Minute Pre-Market Breakout)
Trading Example Between 9:30am to 10:00am

Trading the price action shown would have resulted in a 66% win rate for trades, with 14 winning trades and 7 losing trades.
With 300 shares the potential profit is $768 before deducting $105 in losses.
Losses can vary depending on your risk and reward plan.

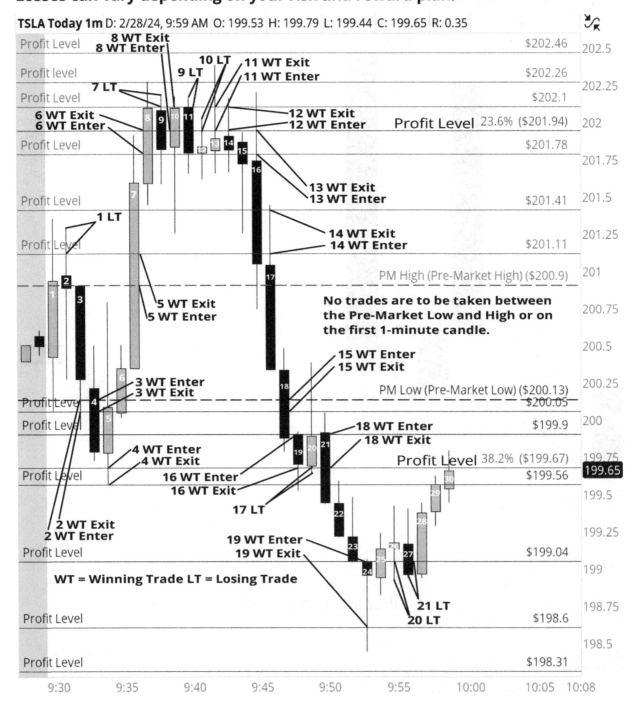

TSLA Today 1m D: 2/28/24, 9:59 AM O: 199.53 H: 199.79 L: 199.44 C: 199.65 R: 0.35

No trades are to be taken between the Pre-Market Low and High or on the first 1-minute candle.

WT = Winning Trade LT = Losing Trade

Trade Description for Open Strategy #2
Example Shown on Page 92

The trade descriptions below show the details of each trade seen in the trading examples. All trades were based on limit orders at the entry and exit of the profit/pivot levels. This assures more exact entries and exits and is important when trying to take profit at tight profit/pivot levels that might be as low as 5 cents.

1. Losing Trade on candle 2
2. Enter a position on candle 3 as it breaks the profit level at $200.13 and the first exit is at the profit level at $200.05
3. Enter a position on candle 4 as it breaks the Pre-Market High at $200.13 and the first exit is at the profit level at $200.05
4. Enter a position on candle 5 as it breaks the profit level at $199.67 and the first exit is at the profit level at $199.56
5. Enter a position on candle 7 as it breaks the Pre-Market High at $200.90 and exit as it breaks the profit level at $201.11
6. Enter a position on candle 8 as it breaks the profit level at $201.78 and the first exit is at the Fibonacci profit level at $201.94
7. Losing Trade on candle 9
8. Enter a position on candle 10 as it breaks the Fibonacci profit level at $201.94 and the first exit is at the profit level at $202.10
9. Losing Trade on candle 11
10. Losing Trade on candle 12
11. Enter a position on candle 13 as it breaks the Fibonacci profit level at $201.94 and the first exit is at the profit level at $202.10
12. Enter a position on candle 14 as it breaks the Fibonacci profit level at $201.94 and the first exit is at the profit level at $202.10
13. Enter a position on candle 16 as it breaks the profit level at $201.78 and the first exit is at the Fibonacci profit level at $201.94
14. Enter a position on candle 17 as it breaks the profit level at $201.11 and the first exit is at the profit level at $201.41
15. Enter a position on candle 18 as it breaks the Pre-Market Low at $200.13 and the first exit is at the profit level at $200.05
16. Enter a position on candle 19 as it breaks the profit level at $199.90 and the first exit is at the Fibonacci profit level at $199.67
17. Losing Trade on candle 20
18. Enter a position on candle 21 as it breaks the profit level at $199.90 and the first exit is at the Fibonacci profit level at $199.67
19. Enter a position on candle 24 as it breaks the profit level at $199.04 and the first exit is at the profit level at $198.60
20. Losing Trade on candle 26
21. Losing Trade on candle 27

A **more aggressive method for taking profits** would be to wait until the price action retraces to the last profit level it breaks through before you exit. This strategy relies heavily on scalping experience but may result in greater profits.

Open Strategy #3
(5 Minute Open Session Breakout)
Complete Setup Example

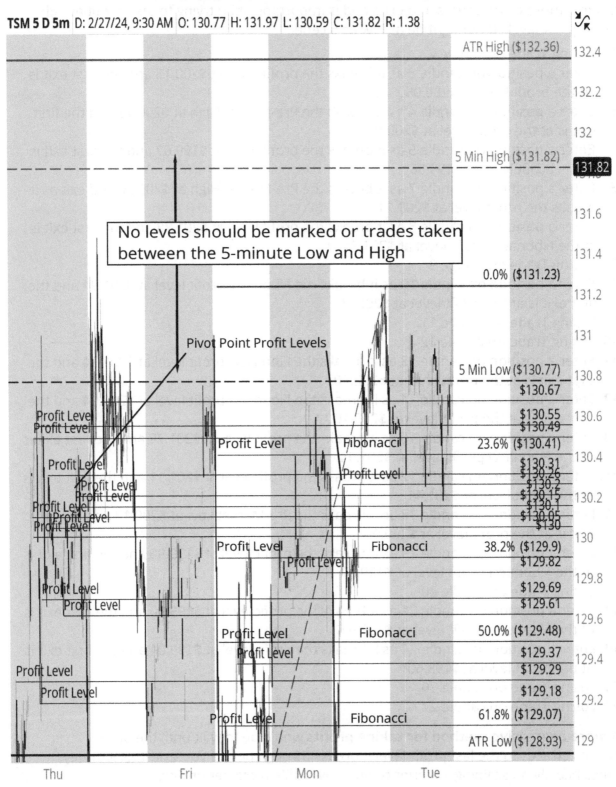

TSM 5 D 5m D: 2/27/24, 9:30 AM O: 130.77 H: 131.97 L: 130.59 C: 131.82 R: 1.38

ATR High ($132.36)

5 Min High ($131.82)

No levels should be marked or trades taken between the 5-minute Low and High

0.0% ($131.23)

Pivot Point Profit Levels

5 Min Low ($130.77)

$130.67

Profit Level
Profit Level

$130.55
$130.49

Profit Level   Fibonacci   23.6% ($130.41)

Profit Level

Profit Level $130.31
$130.26
Profit Level $130.2
Profit Level $130.15
Profit Level $130.1
Profit Level $130.05
Profit Level $130

Profit Level   Fibonacci   38.2% ($129.9)

Profit Level $129.82

Profit Level $129.69

Profit Level $129.61

Profit Level   Fibonacci   50.0% ($129.48)

Profit Level $129.37

Profit Level $129.29

Profit Level $129.18

Profit Level   Fibonacci   61.8% ($129.07)

ATR Low ($128.93)

Thu   Fri   Mon   Tue

Open Strategy #3
(5 Minute Open Session Breakout)
Closeup Example

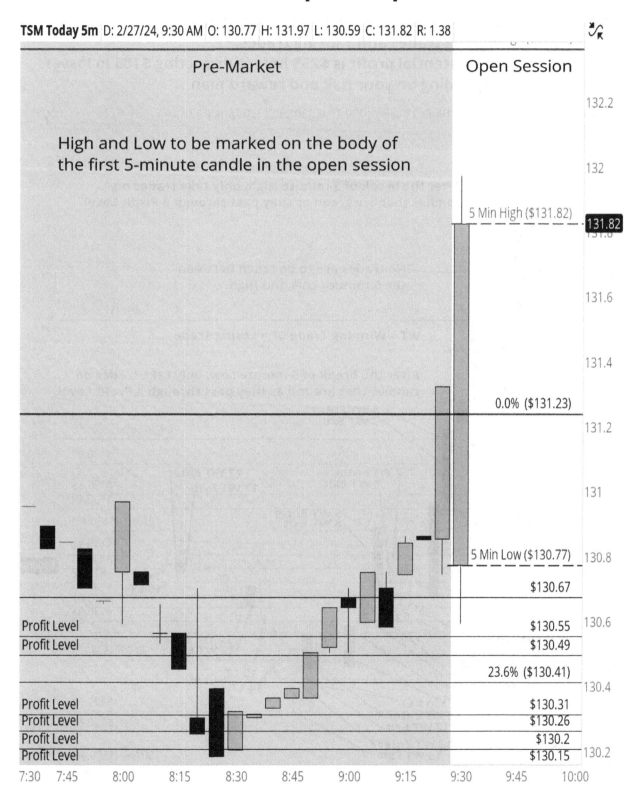

TSM Today 5m D: 2/27/24, 9:30 AM | O: 130.77 | H: 131.97 | L: 130.59 | C: 131.82 | R: 1.38

Pre-Market

Open Session

High and Low to be marked on the body of
the first 5-minute candle in the open session

5 Min High ($131.82)

131.82

0.0% ($131.23)

5 Min Low ($130.77)

$130.67

Profit Level — $130.55

Profit Level — $130.49

23.6% ($130.41)

Profit Level — $130.31

Profit Level — $130.26

Profit Level — $130.2

Profit Level — $130.15

7:30 7:45 8:00 8:15 8:30 8:45 9:00 9:15 9:30 9:45 10:00

Open Strategy #3
(5 Minute Open Session Breakout)
Trading Example From 9:35 to 10:00

Trading the price action shown would have resulted in a 61% win rate for trades, with 11 winning trades and 7 losing trades.
With 300 shares the potential profit is $255 before deducting $105 in losses.
Losses can vary depending on your risk and reward plan.

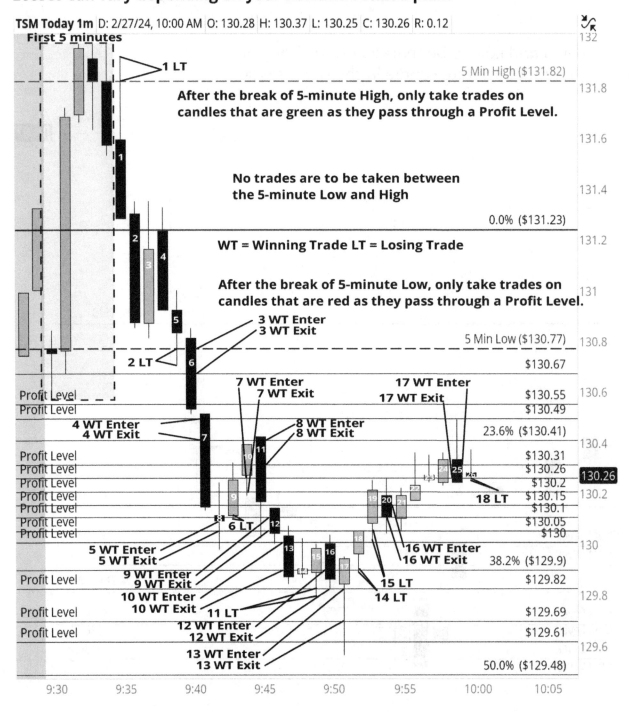

TSM Today 1m D: 2/27/24, 10:00 AM O: 130.28 H: 130.37 L: 130.25 C: 130.26 R: 0.12

First 5 minutes

1 LT

After the break of 5-minute High, only take trades on candles that are green as they pass through a Profit Level.

No trades are to be taken between the 5-minute Low and High

WT = Winning Trade LT = Losing Trade

After the break of 5-minute Low, only take trades on candles that are red as they pass through a Profit Level.

3 WT Enter
3 WT Exit

7 WT Enter
7 WT Exit

17 WT Enter
17 WT Exit

2 LT

4 WT Enter
4 WT Exit

8 WT Enter
8 WT Exit

6 LT

5 WT Enter
5 WT Exit

16 WT Enter
16 WT Exit

18 LT

9 WT Enter
9 WT Exit

10 WT Enter
10 WT Exit

11 LT

15 LT

14 LT

12 WT Enter
12 WT Exit

13 WT Enter
13 WT Exit

Profit Level — 5 Min High ($131.82)
0.0% ($131.23)
5 Min Low ($130.77)
$130.67
$130.55
$130.49
23.6% ($130.41)
$130.31
$130.26
$130.2
$130.15
$130.1
$130.05
$130
38.2% ($129.9)
$129.82
$129.69
$129.61
50.0% ($129.48)

130.26

Trade Description for Open Strategy #3
Example Shown on Page 96

The trade descriptions below show the details of each trade seen in the trading examples. All trades were based on limit orders at the entry and exit of the profit/pivot levels. This assures more exact entries and exits and is important when trying to take profit at tight profit/pivot levels that might be as low as 5 cents.

1. Losing Trade on candle 1
2. Losing Trade on candle 5
3. Enter a position on candle 6 as it breaks the 5-minute Low at $130.77 and the first exit is at the profit level at $130.67
4. Enter a position on candle 7 as it breaks the profit level at $130.49 and the first exit is at the Fibonacci profit level at $130.41
5. Enter a position on candle 8 as it breaks the profit level at $130.10 and the first exit is at the profit level at $130.05
6. Losing Trade on candle 9
7. Enter a position on candle 10 as it breaks the profit level at $130.26 and the first exit is at the Fibonacci profit level at $130.20
8. Enter a position on candle 11 as it breaks the Fibonacci profit level at $130.41 and the first exit is at the profit level at $130.31
9. Enter a position on candle 12 as it breaks the profit level at $130.10 and the first exit is at the pofit level at $130.05
10. Enter a position on candle 13 as it breaks the profit level at 130.00 and the first exit is at the profit level at $129.90
11. Losing Trade on candle 15
12. Enter a position on candle 16 as it breaks the Fibonacci profit level at $129.90 and the first exit is at the profit level at $129.82
13. Enter a position on candle 17 as it breaks the profit level at $129.82 and the first exit is at the profit level at $129.69
14. Losing Trade on candle 18
15. Losing Trade on candle 19
16. Enter a position on candle 20 as it breaks the profit level at $130.15 and the first exit is at the profit level at $130.10
17. Enter a position on candle 25 as it breaks the profit level at $130.31 and the first exit is at the profit level at $130.26
18. Losing Trade on candle 26

A more **aggressive method for taking profits** would be to wait until the price action retraces to the last profit level it breaks through before you exit. This method relies heavily on scalping experience but may lead to greater profits.

Understanding When to Take Your Entries and Exits is key with the Open Strategies

Open Strategy #4
(15 Minute Open Session Breakout)
Complete Setup Example

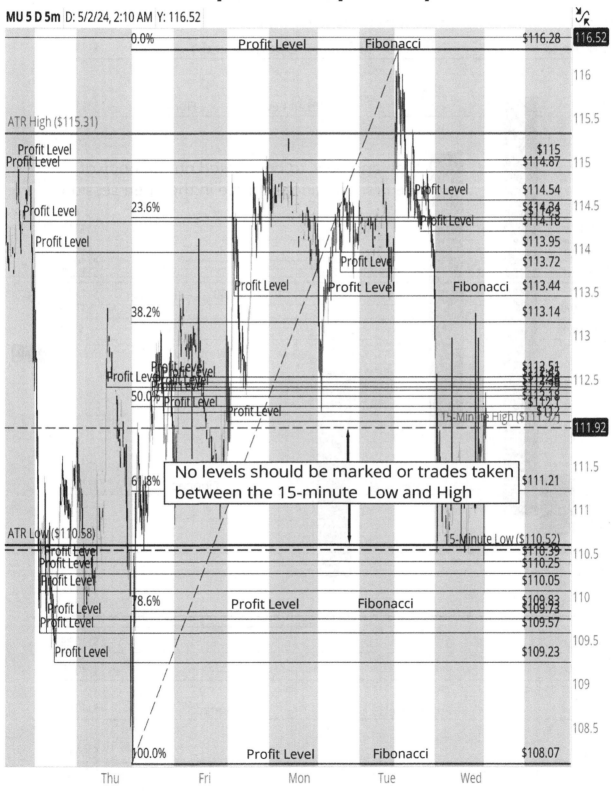

MU 5 D 5m D: 5/2/24, 2:10 AM Y: 116.52

Open Strategy #4
(15 Minute Open Session Breakout Range)
Closeup Example

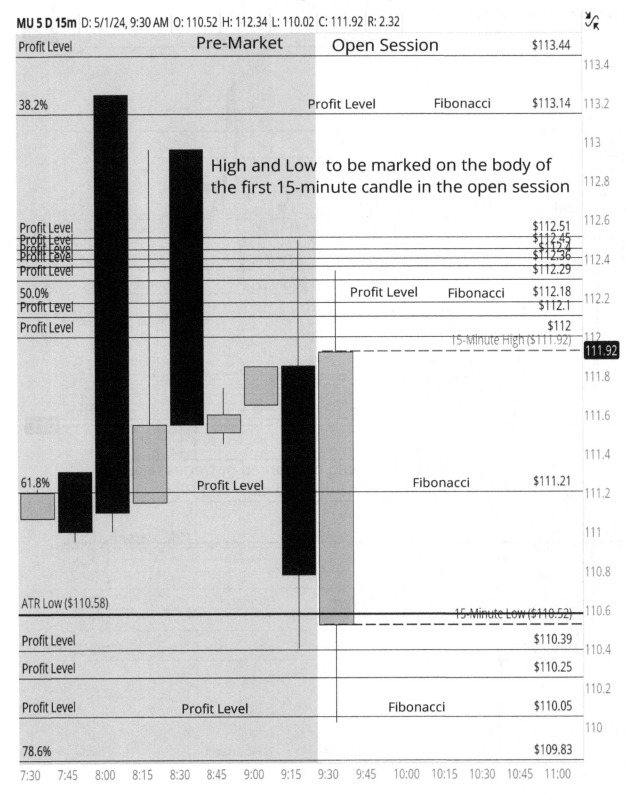

MU 5 D 15m D: 5/1/24, 9:30 AM O: 110.52 H: 112.34 L: 110.02 C: 111.92 R: 2.32

High and Low to be marked on the body of
the first 15-minute candle in the open session

Open Strategy #4
(15 Minute Open Session Breakout)
Trading Example From 9:45 to 10:15

Trading the price action shown would have resulted in a 66% win rate for trades, with 8 winning trades and 4 losing trades.
With 300 shares the potential profit is $267 before deducting $60 in losses.
This can vary depending on your risk and reward plan.

MU 1 D 1m D: 5/1/24, 10:14 AM O: 111.16 H: 111.28 L: 111.05 C: 111.08 R: 0.23

After the break of 15-minute High, only take trades on candles that are green as they pass through a Profit Level.

No trades are to be taken between 15-minute Low and High

After the break of 15-minute Low, only take trades on candles that are red as they pass through a Profit Level.

WT = Winning Trade LT = Losing Trade

Open Strategy #4
(15 Minute Open Session Breakout)
Trading Example From 10:16 to 11:00

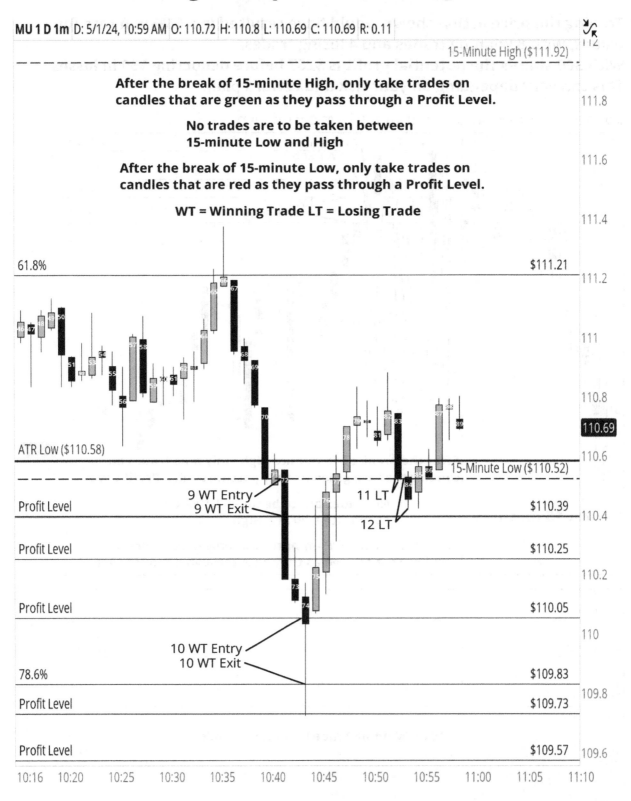

MU 1 D 1m D: 5/1/24, 10:59 AM O: 110.72 H: 110.8 L: 110.69 C: 110.69 R: 0.11

15-Minute High ($111.92)

After the break of 15-minute High, only take trades on candles that are green as they pass through a Profit Level.

No trades are to be taken between 15-minute Low and High

After the break of 15-minute Low, only take trades on candles that are red as they pass through a Profit Level.

WT = Winning Trade LT = Losing Trade

61.8% — $111.21

ATR Low ($110.58)

15-Minute Low ($110.52)

9 WT Entry
9 WT Exit

11 LT

12 LT

Profit Level — $110.39

Profit Level — $110.25

Profit Level — $110.05

10 WT Entry
10 WT Exit

78.6% — $109.83

Profit Level — $109.73

Profit Level — $109.57

Trade Description for Open Strategy #4
Examples Shown on Pages 101 and 102

The trade descriptions below show the details of each trade seen in the trading examples. All trades were based on limit orders at the entry and exit of the profit/pivot levels. This assures more exact entries and exits and is important when trying to take profit at tight profit/pivot levels that might be as low as 5 cents.

1. Enter a position on candle 16 as it breaks the profit level at $112.00 and exit as it breaks the profit level at $112.10

2. Enter a position on candle 17 as it breaks the profit level at $112.10 and exit as it breaks the Fibonacci profit level at $112.18

3. Losing Trade on candle 18

4. Losing Trade on candle 20

5. Enter a position on candle 21 as it breaks the 15-Minute High at $111.92 and exit as it breaks the profit level at $112.00

6. Enter a position on candle 22 as it breaks the profit level at $112.00 and exit as it breaks the profit level at $112.10

7. Enter a position on candle 24 as it breaks the profit level at $112.10 and exit as it breaks the Fibonacci profit level at $112.18

8. Enter a position on candle 26 as it breaks the profit level at $112.00 and exit as it breaks the profit level at $112.10

9. Enter a position on candle 72 as it breaks the 15-Minute Low at $110.52 and exit as it breaks the pofit level at $110.39

10. Enter a position on candle 74 as it breaks the profit level at $110.05 and exit as it breaks the Fibonacci profit level at $109.83

11. Losing Trade on candle 83

12. Losing Trade on candle 84

A **more aggressive method for taking profits** would be to wait until the price action retraces to the last profit level it breaks through before you exit. This method relies heavily on scalping experience but may lead to greater profits.

CHAPTER 8

10 Important Candlestick Patterns for the Open Strategies

The 10 Best Patterns to Look for When Trading the Open Strategies

A new and innovative **rating system** for candlestick patterns was developed by the Million-Dollar Margin Club and released with "**The Candlestick Pattern Playbook"** in late 2023. These ratings were compiled by professional traders to enhance the precision and reliability of using candlestick patterns in stock price predictions. This system quantifies the accuracy of candlestick patterns through rigorous backtesting and cross-comparison with similar rating systems. It is important to note the location of any given pattern within a larger pattern on a chart. That chart's specific time increment may effect the overall accuracy of the pattern's rating.

This rating system utilizes a comprehensive approach including several crucial elements. To initiate the process, an extensive dataset of historical price movements is compiled. This dataset encompasses various stocks, enabling a comprehensive analysis.

Within the historical data set, the rating system identifies and categorizes diverse candlestick patterns, including well-known formations like the bull and bear flags, hammers, bullish engulfing, and shooting stars. The basis of the system is its ability to scrutinize outcomes following the appearance of each candlestick pattern. Each pattern is assessed for its effectiveness in predicting price reversal, continuation of an existing trend, or a breakout into a new trend. The higher rated the candlestick patterns are, the more traders can prioritize them to use in trading strategies, potentially enhancing their success rate.

Candlestick patterns are generally more reliable with higher volume but they should not be considered until <u>after</u> the first 5 minutes of the open due to extreme volatility.

Bull Flag Pattern

Occurs within an uptrend and is characterized by a stong, steep upward move (the flagpole) followed by a consolidation phase of lower volume and relatively smaller price swings than the initial upward move forming a rectangular or parallelogram shape known as the flag.

To trade the bull flag pattern, traders may consider buying the stock when the price breaks above the upper resistance line of the flag, with a stop-loss order placed just below the lower support line. Profit targets can be set by measuring the height of the flagpole and projecting it upward.

This is a Bullish Continuation Pattern

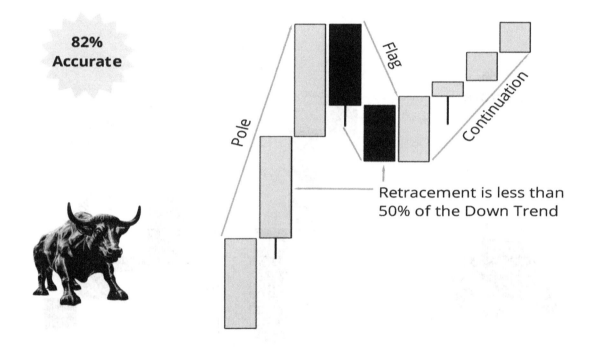

82%
Accurate

Pole

Flag

Continuation

Retracement is less than 50% of the Down Trend

Chart Example of Bull Flag Pattern

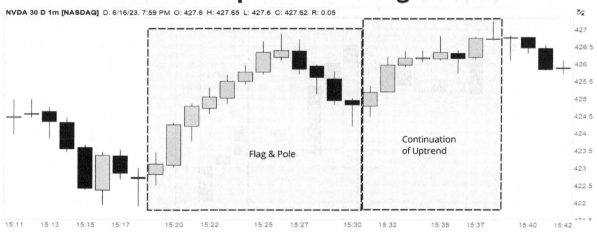

NVDA 30 D 1m [NASDAQ] D: 6/16/23, 7:59 PM O: 427.6 H: 427.65 L: 427.6 C: 427.62 R: 0.05

Flag & Pole

Continuation of Uptrend

Bear Flag Pattern

Occurs within a downtrend and is characterized by a sharp, steep decline in price (known as the flagpole) followed by a consolidation phase with lower volume and relative smaller price swings than the initial decline forming a rectangular or parallelgram shape know as the flag.

To trade the bear flag pattern, traders may consider short-selling the stock when the price breaks below the lower support line of the flag, with a stop loss order placed just above the upper resistance line. Profit targets can be set by measuring the height of the flagpole and projecting it downward.

This is a Bearish Continuation Pattern

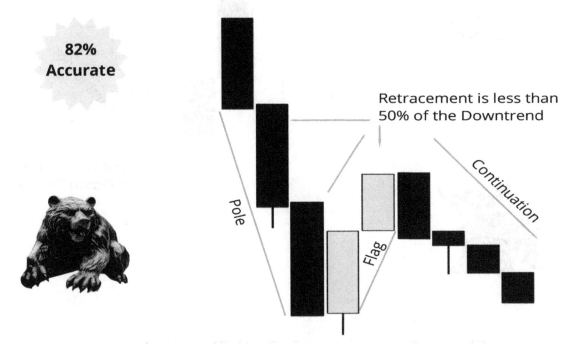

82% Accurate

Retracement is less than 50% of the Downtrend

Pole

Flag

Continuation

Chart Example of Bear Flag Pattern

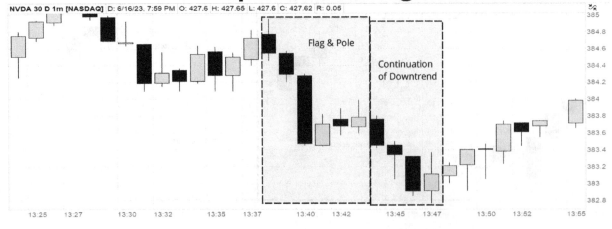

Flat-Top Breakout Pattern

A bullish pattern that occurs when a stock's price breaks through a horizontal resistance level that has been tested by multiple candles, indicating a potential surge in buying pressure and the possibility of continued upward movement. Traders watch for flat-top breakouts as they represent a significant breakout from a price range, capturing the attention of market participants seeking bullish opportunities and potential price increases.

This is a Breakout Pattern.

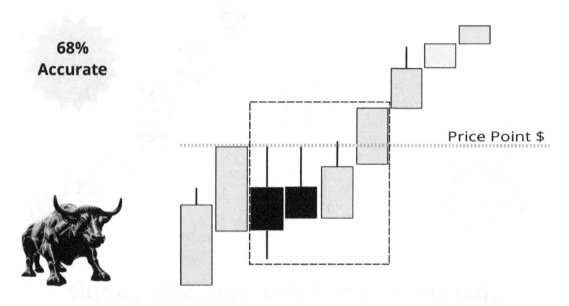

Chart Example of Flat-Top Breakout Pattern

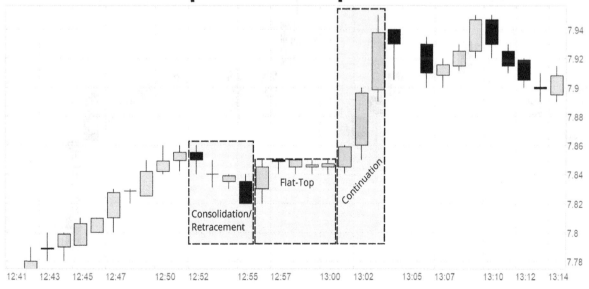

Shooting Star Candle

The Upper Wick is at least twice the length of the Body. It appears after an uptrend and suggests a potential reversal.

This is a Bearish Reversal Pattern.

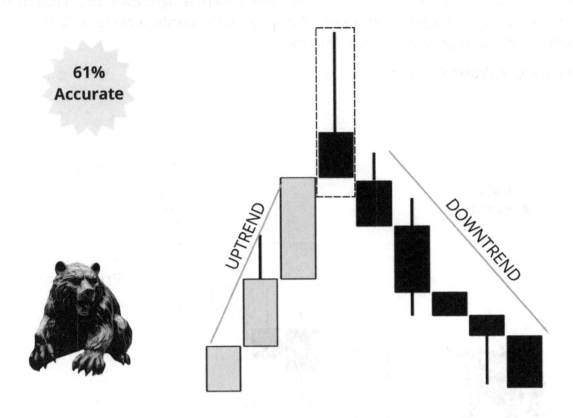

Chart Example of Shooting Star Candle

Bearish Tweezer Top Pattern

This is a two-candlestick formation on stock charts. It consists of two consecutive candles with identical highs, indicating a resistance level. The first candle is bullish, while the second one is bearish, creating a tweezer-like shape. This pattern suggests a potential reversal from an uptrend to a downtrend. It signifies a shift in market sentiment, with selling pressure increasing and buyers losing momentum. Traders often interpret it as a signal to consider short-selling or exiting long positions.

This is a Bearish Reversal Pattern.

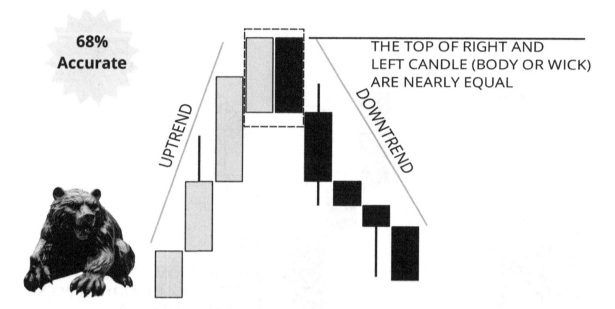

68% Accurate

THE TOP OF RIGHT AND LEFT CANDLE (BODY OR WICK) ARE NEARLY EQUAL

UPTREND

DOWNTREND

Chart Example of a Bearish Tweezer Top Pattern

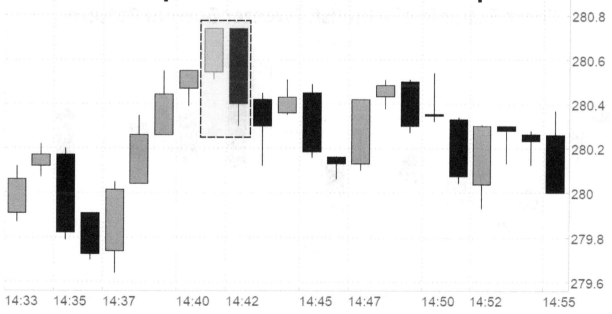

Bullish Tweezer Bottom Pattern

This is a two-candlestick formation on stock charts. It consists of two consecutive candles with identical lows, indicating a support level. The first candle is bearish, while the second one is bullish, creating a tweezer-like shape. This pattern suggests a potential reversal from an downtrend to a uptrend. It signifies a shift in market sentiment, with buying pressure increasing and sellers losing momentum. Traders often interpret it as a signal to consider taking a long position or exiting short positions.

This is a Bullish Reversal Pattern.

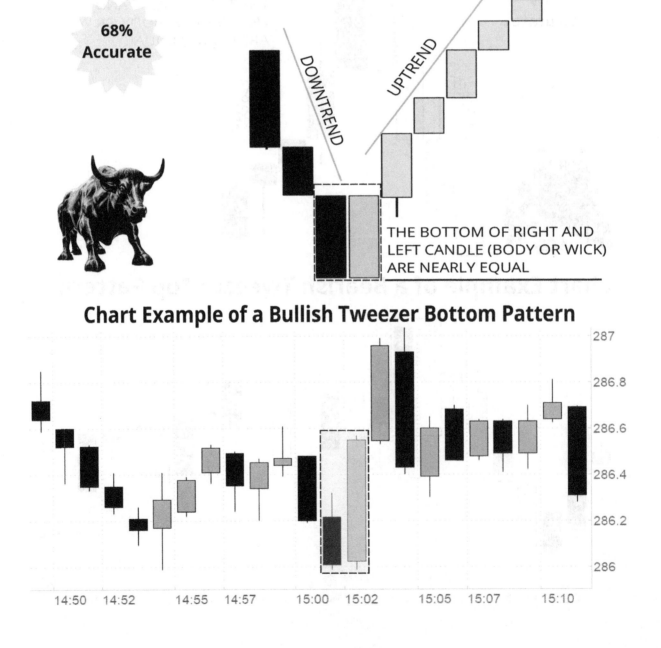

68%
Accurate

DOWNTREND

UPTREND

THE BOTTOM OF RIGHT AND LEFT CANDLE (BODY OR WICK) ARE NEARLY EQUAL

Chart Example of a Bullish Tweezer Bottom Pattern

Hanging Man Candle

The Lower Wick is at least twice the length of the Body. Appearing after an uptrend, it suggests a potential bearish reversal if confirmed by subsequent price action.

This is a Bearish Reversal Pattern

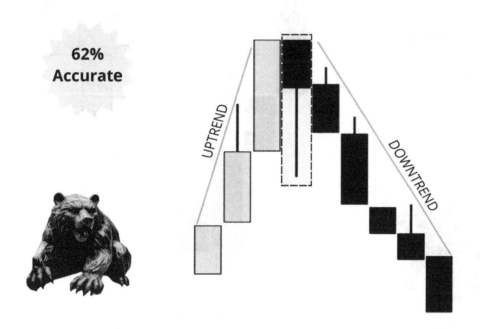

Chart Example of Hanging Man Candle

™

Hammer Candle

The Lower Wick is at least twice the length of the body, appearing after downtrend. It suggests a potential bullish reversal if confirmed by subsequent price action.

This is a Bullish Reversal Pattern.

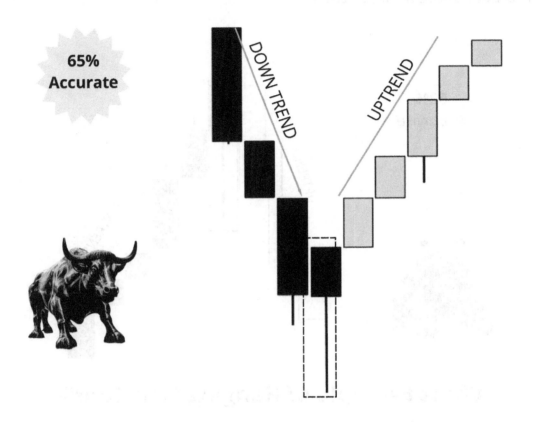

Chart Example of Hammer Candle

Inverted Hammer Candle

The Upper Wick is at least twice the length of the body. It appears after a downtrend and suggests a potential reversal.

This is a Bullish Reversal Pattern

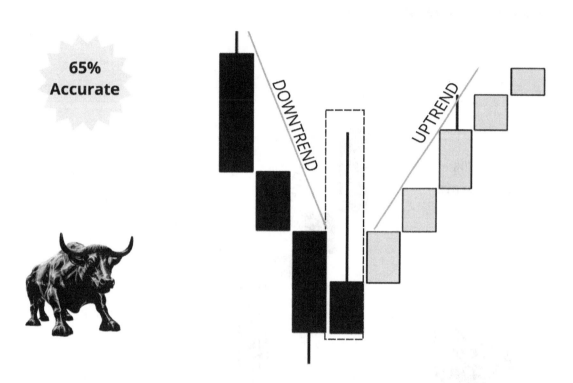

Chart Example of Inverted Hammer Candle

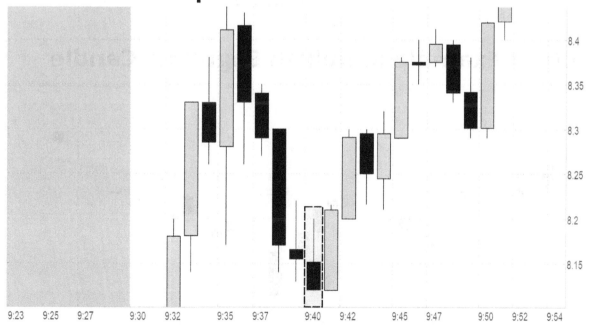

Bullish Engulfing Candle

Consists of two candlesticks and indicates a potential trend reversal. A bullish engulfing pattern occurs when a small bearish candlestick is followed by a larger bullish candlestick that completely engulfs the previous candlestick's body. It suggests a shift from bearish to bullish sentiment.

This is a Bullish Reversal Pattern

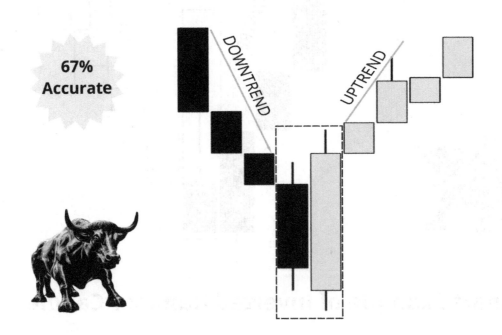

Chart Example of Bullish Engulfing Candle

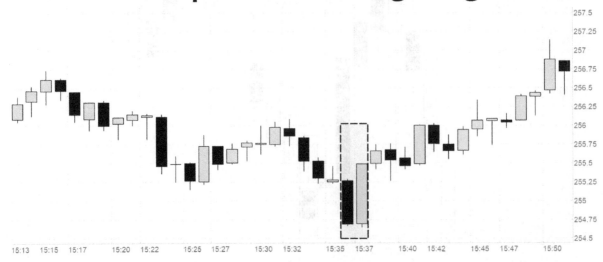

In Conclusion

Remember that success in trading the Open Strategies is not just about mastering charts and strategies. It's about discipline, patience, and fast reactionary skills.

Here are 3 key takeaways to carry with you to trade the Open Strategies:

1. Knowledge is Your Greatest Asset - The more you know about the current market, the better equipped you are to make informed decisions. Continuously monitor the news and stay up-to-date with market developments Breaking news can greatly affect the Open Strategies

2. Risk Management - Protecting your capital should always be your top priority. Use risk management techniques inculding stop-loss orders and a Open Strategy risk management plan with a maximum loss per trade and per day to limit potential losses.

3. Discipline Must Overcome Emotion - Emotional control is essential in trading the Open Strategies. Stick to your trading plan, the breakout and profit/pivot levels and exit strategy, maintain discipline follow the strategy and watch your volume and other indicators.

In conclusion, as you embark on your trading journey while using your **Open Strategies** Watchlist Rating Specifications, Trading Log and your daily Trading Plan pages. Stay focused, stay disciplined, keep updated on news and never forget that every successful trader started as a beginner, faced adversity, and persevered. Your journey will be uniquely yours, but you are not alone. Be confident, you have the potential to achieve your goals and reach the personal empowerment and the financial freedom you seek.

Workbook Tools

- Daily Trading Plan, Watchlist with Rating Specifications Pages and Examples

- Trading Log Pages and Examples

- Weekly Trading Performance record

Additional Watchlist and Rating Specifications, Trading Log, and Weekly Trading Performance Sheets are Available in the Companion Book for DAY TRADING VOL 4.

Daily Guidelines

Date: 1/31/2023

Day: M (T) W TH F | S SU

Trading Plan

Trading the open using premarket breakout range from 7:30-9:15 and trading until 9:45 am

Entry share size per trade 300

My maximum loss per trade allowed $30 and maximum loss per day allowed $100

Always exit my trade if the price action retraces half of the previous 1-min candle

Watchlist with Rating Specifications

Stock Symbol	Stock Name	Breaking News	Today's Breakout Range	Previous Days ATR		Today's Volatility Rating	
AMD	Advance Micro Design	Positive	$ .86	/ 3.00	=	28	%
			$	/	=		%
			$	/	=		%
			$	/	=		%

Summary Notes

AMD had news so I went with the lower ATR today, I always feel safer trading this stock. I took a total of 12 trades in the first 15 mins as per the breakout strategy. They included 8 winning trades and 4 losing trades. I profited a total of $219 dollars.

Trading Log

Date:	Jan. 31, 2023	Symbol:	AMD	Name:	Advance Micro Device

Qty of Shares	Buy/ Sell	Entry Price	Exit Price	Profit/Loss Per Share	Profit/ Loss
300	BUY	$72.60	$72.72	$.12	$36.00

Strategy:

Date:	Jan. 31, 2023	Symbol:	AMD	Name:	Advance Micro Device

Qty of Shares	Buy/ Sell	Entry Price	Exit Price	Profit/Loss Per Share	Profit/ Loss
300	BUY	$72.60	$72.57	$.03	−$9.00

Strategy:

Date:	Jan. 31, 2023	Symbol:	AMD	Name:	Advance Micro Device

Qty of Shares	Buy/ Sell	Entry Price	Exit Price	Profit/Loss Per Share	Profit/ Loss
300	BUY	$72.31	$72.42	$.11	$33.00

Strategy:

Date:	Jan. 31, 2023	Symbol:	AMD	Name:	Advance Micro Device

Qty of Shares	Buy/ Sell	Entry Price	Exit Price	Profit/Loss Per Share	Profit/ Loss
300	BUY	$72.72	$72.90	$.18	$54.00

Strategy:

Date:	Jan. 31, 2023	Symbol:	AMD	Name:	Advance Micro Device

Qty of Shares	Buy/ Sell	Entry Price	Exit Price	Profit/Loss Per Share	Profit/ Loss
300	BUY	$73.04	$73.14	$.10	$30.00

Strategy:
This Example Show 5 of the 12 Trades Taken

Please Review this Book

Dear Reader,

Thank you for purchasing DAY TRADING VOL. 4 "DAY TRADING THE OPEN". Your support means the world to us, and we hope you will enjoyed the journey through these pages.

Reviews are the lifeblood of authors. They help others discover this book and provide valuable feedback for future works. Your thoughts and opinions can make a significant impact.

If you enjoy trading with DAY TRADING VOL 4 and would like to share your thoughts, please leave a review on Amazon (or wherever you purchased this book). Search for DAY TRADING VOL. 4 under your purchases and scroll down to the customer review section. Click "Write a Review" and share your honest thoughts.

If you know someone who might enjoy DAY TRADING VOL. 4, please consider recommending it to them. Word of mouth is incredibly powerful in the world of books.

Thank you once again for choosing to read DAY TRADING VOL. 4, and for considering leaving a review. Your support fuels our interest in writing. We can't wait to hear what you think!

Best Regards,
Million-Dollar Margin Club™ MMCVisions Publishing
YouTube channel: Million-Dollar-Margin Club
million-dollar-marginclub.com

If you would like to join the exclusive Million-Dollar-Margin Club book review and editing program and participate in a unique opportunity, for the details please email:

mmcvisions@gmail.com
with the subject line
Join the MMC

Trading Guidelines and Logs

Daily Guidelines

Date:_____ | Day: M T W TH F | S SU |

Trading Plan
_____
_____
_____
_____
_____
_____
_____
_____
_____
_____

Watchlist with Rating Specifications

Stock Symbol	Stock Name	Breaking News	Today's Breakout Range	Previous Days ATR	Today's Volatility Rating
			$ /	=	%
			$ /	=	%
			$ /	=	%
			$ /	=	%

Summary Notes
_____
_____
_____
_____

Trading Log

Date:		Symbol:		Name:	
Qty of Shares	**Buy/ Sell**	**Entry Price**	**Exit Price**	**Profit/Loss Per Share**	**Profit/ Loss**
Strategy:					

Date:		Symbol:		Name:	
Qty of Shares	**Buy/ Sell**	**Entry Price**	**Exit Price**	**Profit/Loss Per Share**	**Profit/ Loss**
Strategy:					

Date:		Symbol:		Name:	
Qty of Shares	**Buy/ Sell**	**Entry Price**	**Exit Price**	**Profit/Loss Per Share**	**Profit/ Loss**
Strategy:					

Date:		Symbol:		Name:	
Qty of Shares	**Buy/ Sell**	**Entry Price**	**Exit Price**	**Profit/Loss Per Share**	**Profit/ Loss**
Strategy:					

Date:		Symbol:		Name:	
Qty of Shares	**Buy/ Sell**	**Entry Price**	**Exit Price**	**Profit/Loss Per Share**	**Profit/ Loss**
Strategy:					

Daily Guidelines

Date:_____   Day: M T W TH F | S SU

Trading Plan

_____
_____
_____
_____
_____
_____
_____
_____
_____
_____
_____

Watchlist with Rating Specifications

Stock Symbol	Stock Name	Breaking News	Today's Breakout Range	Previous Days ATR	Today's Volatility Rating
			$ /	=	%
			$ /	=	%
			$ /	=	%
			$ /	=	%

Summary Notes

_____
_____
_____
_____

Trading Log

Date:		Symbol:		Name:	
Qty of Shares	Buy/ Sell	Entry Price	Exit Price	Profit/Loss Per Share	Profit/ Loss
Strategy:					

Date:		Symbol:		Name:	
Qty of Shares	Buy/ Sell	Entry Price	Exit Price	Profit/Loss Per Share	Profit/ Loss
Strategy:					

Date:		Symbol:		Name:	
Qty of Shares	Buy/ Sell	Entry Price	Exit Price	Profit/Loss Per Share	Profit/ Loss
Strategy:					

Date:		Symbol:		Name:	
Qty of Shares	Buy/ Sell	Entry Price	Exit Price	Profit/Loss Per Share	Profit/ Loss
Strategy:					

Date:		Symbol:		Name:	
Qty of Shares	Buy/ Sell	Entry Price	Exit Price	Profit/Loss Per Share	Profit/ Loss
Strategy:					

Daily Guidelines

Date:_____ Day: M T W TH F | S SU

Trading Plan

Watchlist with Rating Specifications

Stock Symbol	Stock Name	Breaking News	Today's Breakout Range	Previous Days ATR	Today's Volatility Rating
			$ /	=	%
			$ /	=	%
			$ /	=	%
			$ /	=	%

Summary Notes

Trading Log

Date:		Symbol:		Name:	
Qty of Shares	Buy/ Sell	Entry Price	Exit Price	Profit/Loss Per Share	Profit/ Loss
Strategy:					

Date:		Symbol:		Name:	
Qty of Shares	Buy/ Sell	Entry Price	Exit Price	Profit/Loss Per Share	Profit/ Loss
Strategy:					

Date:		Symbol:		Name:	
Qty of Shares	Buy/ Sell	Entry Price	Exit Price	Profit/Loss Per Share	Profit/ Loss
Strategy:					

Date:		Symbol:		Name:	
Qty of Shares	Buy/ Sell	Entry Price	Exit Price	Profit/Loss Per Share	Profit/ Loss
Strategy:					

Date:		Symbol:		Name:	
Qty of Shares	Buy/ Sell	Entry Price	Exit Price	Profit/Loss Per Share	Profit/ Loss
Strategy:					

Daily Guidelines

Date:_____   Day: M T W TH F | S SU

Trading Plan

Watchlist with Rating Specifications

Stock Symbol	Stock Name	Breaking News	Today's Breakout Range	Previous Days ATR	Today's Volatility Rating
			$ /	=	%
			$ /	=	%
			$ /	=	%
			$ /	=	%

Summary Notes

Trading Log

Date:		Symbol:		Name:	
Qty of Shares	Buy/ Sell	Entry Price	Exit Price	Profit/Loss Per Share	Profit/ Loss
Strategy:					

Date:		Symbol:		Name:	
Qty of Shares	Buy/ Sell	Entry Price	Exit Price	Profit/Loss Per Share	Profit/ Loss
Strategy:					

Date:		Symbol:		Name:	
Qty of Shares	Buy/ Sell	Entry Price	Exit Price	Profit/Loss Per Share	Profit/ Loss
Strategy:					

Date:		Symbol:		Name:	
Qty of Shares	Buy/ Sell	Entry Price	Exit Price	Profit/Loss Per Share	Profit/ Loss
Strategy:					

Date:		Symbol:		Name:	
Qty of Shares	Buy/ Sell	Entry Price	Exit Price	Profit/Loss Per Share	Profit/ Loss
Strategy:					

Daily Guidelines

Date:_____   Day: M T W TH F | S SU

Trading Plan

Watchlist with Rating Specifications					
Stock Symbol	Stock Name	Breaking News	Today's Breakout Range	Previous Days ATR	Today's Volatility Rating
			$ /	=	%
			$ /	=	%
			$ /	=	%
			$ /	=	%

Summary Notes

Trading Log

Date:		Symbol:		Name:	
Qty of Shares	Buy/ Sell	Entry Price	Exit Price	Profit/Loss Per Share	Profit/ Loss
Strategy:					

Date:		Symbol:		Name:	
Qty of Shares	Buy/ Sell	Entry Price	Exit Price	Profit/Loss Per Share	Profit/ Loss
Strategy:					

Date:		Symbol:		Name:	
Qty of Shares	Buy/ Sell	Entry Price	Exit Price	Profit/Loss Per Share	Profit/ Loss
Strategy:					

Date:		Symbol:		Name:	
Qty of Shares	Buy/ Sell	Entry Price	Exit Price	Profit/Loss Per Share	Profit/ Loss
Strategy:					

Date:		Symbol:		Name:	
Qty of Shares	Buy/ Sell	Entry Price	Exit Price	Profit/Loss Per Share	Profit/ Loss
Strategy:					

Daily Guidelines

Date:_____ | Day: M T W TH F | S SU

Trading Plan

Watchlist with Rating Specifications

Stock Symbol	Stock Name	Breaking News	Today's Breakout Range	Previous Days ATR	Today's Volatility Rating
			$ /	=	%
			$ /	=	%
			$ /	=	%
			$ /	=	%

Summary Notes

Trading Log

Date:		Symbol:		Name:	
Qty of Shares	Buy/ Sell	Entry Price	Exit Price	Profit/Loss Per Share	Profit/ Loss
Strategy:					

Date:		Symbol:		Name:	
Qty of Shares	Buy/ Sell	Entry Price	Exit Price	Profit/Loss Per Share	Profit/ Loss
Strategy:					

Date:		Symbol:		Name:	
Qty of Shares	Buy/ Sell	Entry Price	Exit Price	Profit/Loss Per Share	Profit/ Loss
Strategy:					

Date:		Symbol:		Name:	
Qty of Shares	Buy/ Sell	Entry Price	Exit Price	Profit/Loss Per Share	Profit/ Loss
Strategy:					

Date:		Symbol:		Name:	
Qty of Shares	Buy/ Sell	Entry Price	Exit Price	Profit/Loss Per Share	Profit/ Loss
Strategy:					

Daily Guidelines

Date:_____   Day: M T W TH F | S SU

Trading Plan

Watchlist with Rating Specifications

Stock Symbol	Stock Name	Breaking News	Today's Breakout Range	Previous Days ATR	Today's Volatility Rating
			$ /	=	%
			$ /	=	%
			$ /	=	%
			$ /	=	%

Summary Notes

Trading Log

Date:		Symbol:		Name:	
Qty of Shares	Buy/ Sell	Entry Price	Exit Price	Profit/Loss Per Share	Profit/ Loss
Strategy:					

Date:		Symbol:		Name:	
Qty of Shares	Buy/ Sell	Entry Price	Exit Price	Profit/Loss Per Share	Profit/ Loss
Strategy:					

Date:		Symbol:		Name:	
Qty of Shares	Buy/ Sell	Entry Price	Exit Price	Profit/Loss Per Share	Profit/ Loss
Strategy:					

Date:		Symbol:		Name:	
Qty of Shares	Buy/ Sell	Entry Price	Exit Price	Profit/Loss Per Share	Profit/ Loss
Strategy:					

Date:		Symbol:		Name:	
Qty of Shares	Buy/ Sell	Entry Price	Exit Price	Profit/Loss Per Share	Profit/ Loss
Strategy:					

Daily Guidelines

Date:_____   Day: M T W TH F | S SU

Trading Plan

Watchlist with Rating Specifications

Stock Symbol	Stock Name	Breaking News	Today's Breakout Range	Previous Days ATR	Today's Volatility Rating
			$ /	=	%
			$ /	=	%
			$ /	=	%
			$ /	=	%

Summary Notes

Trading Log

Date:		Symbol:		Name:	
Qty of Shares	Buy/ Sell	Entry Price	Exit Price	Profit/Loss Per Share	Profit/ Loss
Strategy:					

Date:		Symbol:		Name:	
Qty of Shares	Buy/ Sell	Entry Price	Exit Price	Profit/Loss Per Share	Profit/ Loss
Strategy:					

Date:		Symbol:		Name:	
Qty of Shares	Buy/ Sell	Entry Price	Exit Price	Profit/Loss Per Share	Profit/ Loss
Strategy:					

Date:		Symbol:		Name:	
Qty of Shares	Buy/ Sell	Entry Price	Exit Price	Profit/Loss Per Share	Profit/ Loss
Strategy:					

Date:		Symbol:		Name:	
Qty of Shares	Buy/ Sell	Entry Price	Exit Price	Profit/Loss Per Share	Profit/ Loss
Strategy:					

Daily Guidelines

Date:_____ Day: M T W TH F | S SU

Trading Plan

Watchlist with Rating Specifications

Stock Symbol	Stock Name	Breaking News	Today's Breakout Range	Previous Days ATR	Today's Volatility Rating
			$ / =		%
			$ / =		%
			$ / =		%
			$ / =		%

Summary Notes

Trading Log

Date:		Symbol:		Name:	
Qty of Shares	Buy/ Sell	Entry Price	Exit Price	Profit/Loss Per Share	Profit/ Loss
Strategy:					

Date:		Symbol:		Name:	
Qty of Shares	Buy/ Sell	Entry Price	Exit Price	Profit/Loss Per Share	Profit/ Loss
Strategy:					

Date:		Symbol:		Name:	
Qty of Shares	Buy/ Sell	Entry Price	Exit Price	Profit/Loss Per Share	Profit/ Loss
Strategy:					

Date:		Symbol:		Name:	
Qty of Shares	Buy/ Sell	Entry Price	Exit Price	Profit/Loss Per Share	Profit/ Loss
Strategy:					

Date:		Symbol:		Name:	
Qty of Shares	Buy/ Sell	Entry Price	Exit Price	Profit/Loss Per Share	Profit/ Loss
Strategy:					

Daily Guidelines

Date:_____ Day: M T W TH F | S SU

Trading Plan

_____
_____
_____
_____
_____
_____
_____
_____
_____
_____

Watchlist with Rating Specifications

Stock Symbol	Stock Name	Breaking News	Today's Breakout Range	Previous Days ATR	Today's Volatility Rating
			$ /	=	%
			$ /	=	%
			$ /	=	%
			$ /	=	%

Summary Notes

_____
_____
_____
_____

Trading Log

Date:		Symbol:		Name:	
Qty of Shares	**Buy/ Sell**	**Entry Price**	**Exit Price**	**Profit/Loss Per Share**	**Profit/ Loss**
Strategy:					

Date:		Symbol:		Name:	
Qty of Shares	**Buy/ Sell**	**Entry Price**	**Exit Price**	**Profit/Loss Per Share**	**Profit/ Loss**
Strategy:					

Date:		Symbol:		Name:	
Qty of Shares	**Buy/ Sell**	**Entry Price**	**Exit Price**	**Profit/Loss Per Share**	**Profit/ Loss**
Strategy:					

Date:		Symbol:		Name:	
Qty of Shares	**Buy/ Sell**	**Entry Price**	**Exit Price**	**Profit/Loss Per Share**	**Profit/ Loss**
Strategy:					

Date:		Symbol:		Name:	
Qty of Shares	**Buy/ Sell**	**Entry Price**	**Exit Price**	**Profit/Loss Per Share**	**Profit/ Loss**
Strategy:					

Daily Guidelines

Date:_____   Day: M T W TH F | S SU

Trading Plan

Watchlist with Rating Specifications

Stock Symbol	Stock Name	Breaking News	Today's Breakout Range	Previous Days ATR	Today's Volatility Rating
			$ /	=	%
			$ /	=	%
			$ /	=	%
			$ /	=	%

Summary Notes

Trading Log

Date:		Symbol:		Name:	
Qty of Shares	Buy/ Sell	Entry Price	Exit Price	Profit/Loss Per Share	Profit/ Loss
Strategy:					

Date:		Symbol:		Name:	
Qty of Shares	Buy/ Sell	Entry Price	Exit Price	Profit/Loss Per Share	Profit/ Loss
Strategy:					

Date:		Symbol:		Name:	
Qty of Shares	Buy/ Sell	Entry Price	Exit Price	Profit/Loss Per Share	Profit/ Loss
Strategy:					

Date:		Symbol:		Name:	
Qty of Shares	Buy/ Sell	Entry Price	Exit Price	Profit/Loss Per Share	Profit/ Loss
Strategy:					

Date:		Symbol:		Name:	
Qty of Shares	Buy/ Sell	Entry Price	Exit Price	Profit/Loss Per Share	Profit/ Loss
Strategy:					

Daily Guidelines

Date:_____   Day: M T W TH F | S SU

Trading Plan

Watchlist with Rating Specifications					
Stock Symbol	Stock Name	Breaking News	Today's Breakout Range	Previous Days ATR	Today's Volatility Rating
			$ / =		%
			$ / =		%
			$ / =		%
			$ / =		%

Summary Notes

Trading Log

Date:		Symbol:		Name:	
Qty of Shares	Buy/ Sell	Entry Price	Exit Price	Profit/Loss Per Share	Profit/ Loss
Strategy:					

Date:		Symbol:		Name:	
Qty of Shares	Buy/ Sell	Entry Price	Exit Price	Profit/Loss Per Share	Profit/ Loss
Strategy:					

Date:		Symbol:		Name:	
Qty of Shares	Buy/ Sell	Entry Price	Exit Price	Profit/Loss Per Share	Profit/ Loss
Strategy:					

Date:		Symbol:		Name:	
Qty of Shares	Buy/ Sell	Entry Price	Exit Price	Profit/Loss Per Share	Profit/ Loss
Strategy:					

Date:		Symbol:		Name:	
Qty of Shares	Buy/ Sell	Entry Price	Exit Price	Profit/Loss Per Share	Profit/ Loss
Strategy:					

Daily Guidelines

Date:_____

| Day: M T W TH F | S SU |

Trading Plan

_____
_____
_____
_____
_____
_____
_____
_____
_____
_____

Watchlist with Rating Specifications

Stock Symbol	Stock Name	Breaking News	Today's Breakout Range	Previous Days ATR	Today's Volatility Rating
			$ /	=	%
			$ /	=	%
			$ /	=	%
			$ /	=	%

Summary Notes

_____
_____
_____
_____

Trading Log

Date:		Symbol:		Name:	

Qty of Shares	Buy/ Sell	Entry Price	Exit Price	Profit/Loss Per Share	Profit/ Loss

Strategy:

Date:		Symbol:		Name:	

Qty of Shares	Buy/ Sell	Entry Price	Exit Price	Profit/Loss Per Share	Profit/ Loss

Strategy:

Date:		Symbol:		Name:	

Qty of Shares	Buy/ Sell	Entry Price	Exit Price	Profit/Loss Per Share	Profit/ Loss

Strategy:

Date:		Symbol:		Name:	

Qty of Shares	Buy/ Sell	Entry Price	Exit Price	Profit/Loss Per Share	Profit/ Loss

Strategy:

Date:		Symbol:		Name:	

Qty of Shares	Buy/ Sell	Entry Price	Exit Price	Profit/Loss Per Share	Profit/ Loss

Strategy:

Daily Guidelines

Date:_____   Day: M T W TH F | S SU

Trading Plan

_____
_____
_____
_____
_____
_____
_____
_____
_____
_____

Watchlist with Rating Specifications

Stock Symbol	Stock Name	Breaking News	Today's Breakout Range	Previous Days ATR	Today's Volatility Rating
			$ /	=	%
			$ /	=	%
			$ /	=	%
			$ /	=	%

Summary Notes

_____
_____
_____
_____

Trading Log

Date:		Symbol:		Name:	
Qty of Shares	Buy/ Sell	Entry Price	Exit Price	Profit/Loss Per Share	Profit/ Loss
Strategy:					

Date:		Symbol:		Name:	
Qty of Shares	Buy/ Sell	Entry Price	Exit Price	Profit/Loss Per Share	Profit/ Loss
Strategy:					

Date:		Symbol:		Name:	
Qty of Shares	Buy/ Sell	Entry Price	Exit Price	Profit/Loss Per Share	Profit/ Loss
Strategy:					

Date:		Symbol:		Name:	
Qty of Shares	Buy/ Sell	Entry Price	Exit Price	Profit/Loss Per Share	Profit/ Loss
Strategy:					

Date:		Symbol:		Name:	
Qty of Shares	Buy/ Sell	Entry Price	Exit Price	Profit/Loss Per Share	Profit/ Loss
Strategy:					

Daily Guidelines

Date:_____ Day: M T W TH F | S SU

Trading Plan

_____
_____
_____
_____
_____
_____
_____
_____
_____
_____

Watchlist with Rating Specifications

Stock Symbol	Stock Name	Breaking News	Today's Breakout Range	Previous Days ATR	Today's Volatility Rating
			$ /	=	%
			$ /	=	%
			$ /	=	%
			$ /	=	%

Summary Notes

_____
_____
_____
_____

Trading Log

Date:		Symbol:		Name:	
Qty of Shares	Buy/ Sell	Entry Price	Exit Price	Profit/Loss Per Share	Profit/ Loss
Strategy:					

Date:		Symbol:		Name:	
Qty of Shares	Buy/ Sell	Entry Price	Exit Price	Profit/Loss Per Share	Profit/ Loss
Strategy:					

Date:		Symbol:		Name:	
Qty of Shares	Buy/ Sell	Entry Price	Exit Price	Profit/Loss Per Share	Profit/ Loss
Strategy:					

Date:		Symbol:		Name:	
Qty of Shares	Buy/ Sell	Entry Price	Exit Price	Profit/Loss Per Share	Profit/ Loss
Strategy:					

Date:		Symbol:		Name:	
Qty of Shares	Buy/ Sell	Entry Price	Exit Price	Profit/Loss Per Share	Profit/ Loss
Strategy:					

Daily Guidelines

Date:_____ Day: M T W TH F | S SU

Trading Plan

_____
_____
_____
_____
_____
_____
_____
_____
_____
_____
_____

Watchlist with Rating Specifications

Stock Symbol	Stock Name	Breaking News	Today's Breakout Range	Previous Days ATR	Today's Volatility Rating
			$ /	=	%
			$ /	=	%
			$ /	=	%
			$ /	=	%

Summary Notes

_____
_____
_____
_____

Trading Log

Date:		Symbol:		Name:	
Qty of Shares	**Buy/ Sell**	**Entry Price**	**Exit Price**	**Profit/Loss Per Share**	**Profit/ Loss**
Strategy:					

Date:		Symbol:		Name:	
Qty of Shares	**Buy/ Sell**	**Entry Price**	**Exit Price**	**Profit/Loss Per Share**	**Profit/ Loss**
Strategy:					

Date:		Symbol:		Name:	
Qty of Shares	**Buy/ Sell**	**Entry Price**	**Exit Price**	**Profit/Loss Per Share**	**Profit/ Loss**
Strategy:					

Date:		Symbol:		Name:	
Qty of Shares	**Buy/ Sell**	**Entry Price**	**Exit Price**	**Profit/Loss Per Share**	**Profit/ Loss**
Strategy:					

Date:		Symbol:		Name:	
Qty of Shares	**Buy/ Sell**	**Entry Price**	**Exit Price**	**Profit/Loss Per Share**	**Profit/ Loss**
Strategy:					

Daily Guidelines

Date:_____   Day: M T W TH F | S SU

Trading Plan

_____
_____
_____
_____
_____
_____
_____
_____
_____
_____

Watchlist with Rating Specifications

Stock Symbol	Stock Name	Breaking News	Today's Breakout Range	Previous Days ATR	Today's Volatility Rating
			$ /	=	%
			$ /	=	%
			$ /	=	%
			$ /	=	%

Summary Notes

_____
_____
_____
_____

Trading Log

Date:		Symbol:		Name:	
Qty of Shares	Buy/ Sell	Entry Price	Exit Price	Profit/Loss Per Share	Profit/ Loss
Strategy:					

Date:		Symbol:		Name:	
Qty of Shares	Buy/ Sell	Entry Price	Exit Price	Profit/Loss Per Share	Profit/ Loss
Strategy:					

Date:		Symbol:		Name:	
Qty of Shares	Buy/ Sell	Entry Price	Exit Price	Profit/Loss Per Share	Profit/ Loss
Strategy:					

Date:		Symbol:		Name:	
Qty of Shares	Buy/ Sell	Entry Price	Exit Price	Profit/Loss Per Share	Profit/ Loss
Strategy:					

Date:		Symbol:		Name:	
Qty of Shares	Buy/ Sell	Entry Price	Exit Price	Profit/Loss Per Share	Profit/ Loss
Strategy:					

Daily Guidelines

Date:_____   Day: M T W TH F │ S SU

Trading Plan

_____
_____
_____
_____
_____
_____
_____
_____
_____
_____
_____

Watchlist with Rating Specifications

Stock Symbol	Stock Name	Breaking News	Today's Breakout Range	Previous Days ATR	Today's Volatility Rating
			$ /	=	%
			$ /	=	%
			$ /	=	%
			$ /	=	%

Summary Notes

_____
_____
_____
_____

Trading Log

Date:		Symbol:		Name:	
Qty of Shares	Buy/ Sell	Entry Price	Exit Price	Profit/Loss Per Share	Profit/ Loss
Strategy:					

Date:		Symbol:		Name:	
Qty of Shares	Buy/ Sell	Entry Price	Exit Price	Profit/Loss Per Share	Profit/ Loss
Strategy:					

Date:		Symbol:		Name:	
Qty of Shares	Buy/ Sell	Entry Price	Exit Price	Profit/Loss Per Share	Profit/ Loss
Strategy:					

Date:		Symbol:		Name:	
Qty of Shares	Buy/ Sell	Entry Price	Exit Price	Profit/Loss Per Share	Profit/ Loss
Strategy:					

Date:		Symbol:		Name:	
Qty of Shares	Buy/ Sell	Entry Price	Exit Price	Profit/Loss Per Share	Profit/ Loss
Strategy:					

Daily Guidelines

Date:_____ | Day: M T W TH F | S SU |

Trading Plan

_____
_____
_____
_____
_____
_____
_____
_____
_____
_____

Watchlist with Rating Specifications

Stock Symbol	Stock Name	Breaking News	Today's Breakout Range	Previous Days ATR	Today's Volatility Rating
			$ /	=	%
			$ /	=	%
			$ /	=	%
			$ /	=	%

Summary Notes

_____
_____
_____
_____

Trading Log

Date:		Symbol:		Name:	
Qty of Shares	Buy/ Sell	Entry Price	Exit Price	Profit/Loss Per Share	Profit/ Loss
Strategy:					

Date:		Symbol:		Name:	
Qty of Shares	Buy/ Sell	Entry Price	Exit Price	Profit/Loss Per Share	Profit/ Loss
Strategy:					

Date:		Symbol:		Name:	
Qty of Shares	Buy/ Sell	Entry Price	Exit Price	Profit/Loss Per Share	Profit/ Loss
Strategy:					

Date:		Symbol:		Name:	
Qty of Shares	Buy/ Sell	Entry Price	Exit Price	Profit/Loss Per Share	Profit/ Loss
Strategy:					

Date:		Symbol:		Name:	
Qty of Shares	Buy/ Sell	Entry Price	Exit Price	Profit/Loss Per Share	Profit/ Loss
Strategy:					

Daily Guidelines

Date:_____   Day: M T W TH F | S SU

Trading Plan

_____
_____
_____
_____
_____
_____
_____
_____
_____
_____

Watchlist with Rating Specifications

Stock Symbol	Stock Name	Breaking News	Today's Breakout Range	Previous Days ATR	Today's Volatility Rating
			$ /	=	%
			$ /	=	%
			$ /	=	%
			$ /	=	%

Summary Notes

_____
_____
_____
_____

Trading Log

Date:		Symbol:		Name:	
Qty of Shares	Buy/ Sell	Entry Price	Exit Price	Profit/Loss Per Share	Profit/ Loss
Strategy:					

Date:		Symbol:		Name:	
Qty of Shares	Buy/ Sell	Entry Price	Exit Price	Profit/Loss Per Share	Profit/ Loss
Strategy:					

Date:		Symbol:		Name:	
Qty of Shares	Buy/ Sell	Entry Price	Exit Price	Profit/Loss Per Share	Profit/ Loss
Strategy:					

Date:		Symbol:		Name:	
Qty of Shares	Buy/ Sell	Entry Price	Exit Price	Profit/Loss Per Share	Profit/ Loss
Strategy:					

Date:		Symbol:		Name:	
Qty of Shares	Buy/ Sell	Entry Price	Exit Price	Profit/Loss Per Share	Profit/ Loss
Strategy:					

Weekly Trading Performance Record

Week of	Monday	Tuesday	Wednesday	Thursday	Friday	Weekly
	Goal $ Actual $	Goal $ Actual $	Goal $ Actual $	Goal $ Actual $	Goal $ Actual $	Goal $ Actual $
	Goal $ Actual $	Goal $ Actual $	Goal $ Actual $	Goal $ Actual $	Goal $ Actual $	Goal $ Actual $
	Goal $ Actual $	Goal $ Actual $	Goal $ Actual $	Goal $ Actual $	Goal $ Actual $	Goal $ Actual $
	Goal $ Actual $	Goal $ Actual $	Goal $ Actual $	Goal $ Actual $	Goal $ Actual $	Goal $ Actual $
	Goal $ Actual $	Goal $ Actual $	Goal $ Actual $	Goal $ Actual $	Goal $ Actual $	Goal $ Actual $
	Goal $ Actual $	Goal $ Actual $	Goal $ Actual $	Goal $ Actual $	Goal $ Actual $	Goal $ Actual $
	Goal $ Actual $	Goal $ Actual $	Goal $ Actual $	Goal $ Actual $	Goal $ Actual $	Goal $ Actual $
	Goal $ Actual $	Goal $ Actual $	Goal $ Actual $	Goal $ Actual $	Goal $ Actual $	Goal $ Actual $
	Goal $ Actual $	Goal $ Actual $	Goal $ Actual $	Goal $ Actual $	Goal $ Actual $	Goal $ Actual $
	Goal $ Actual $	Goal $ Actual $	Goal $ Actual $	Goal $ Actual $	Goal $ Actual $	Goal $ Actual $

10 Weeks $_____

_____

_____

_____

_____

_____

Glossary of Common Trading Terms

- **Average True Range (ATR)** - measures volatility and price range over time
- **Bear Market** - prolonged period of declining stock prices
- **Breakout** - price moves outside a defined support/resistance level
- **Breakout Range** - defined price range from which a breakout occurs
- **Breakout Volume** - increased trading volume during price breakout
- **Brokerage** - firm facilitating buying and selling of securities
- **Bull Market** - prolonged period of rising stock prices
- **Candlestick Chart** - visual representation of price movements
- **Candlestick Patterns** - graphical formation representing price movements
- **Consolidation** - period of stable prices before a breakout
- **Day Trading** - buying and selling within the same day
- **Direct Access** - trading platform with direct market access
- **Exponential Moving Average (EMA)** - weighted average giving more importance to recent price data
- **Fibonacci Retracement** - potential support/resistance levels based on Fibonacci sequence
- **High** - highest price reached during a trading period
- **Level II** - detailed view of open buy/sell orders
- **Low** - lowest price reached during a trading period
- **Margin Account** - brokerage account allowing buying on margin
- **Market Orders** - buy/sell orders executed immediately at current price
- **Momentum Indicators** - indicators measuring the speed of price movements
- **Moving Average Convergence Divergence (MACD)** - trend-following momentum indicator
- **National Best Bid and Offer (NBBO)** - best available bid/ask prices nationally
- **News** - current events impacting stock prices
- **Open/Closing Price** - intial/final price of a stock during open session
- **Open Strategy #1** - marked out at 7:30-9:15 am US ET premarket high and low
- **Open Strategy #2** - marked out at 8:30-9:00 am US ET premarket high and low
- **Open Strategy #3** - mark high and low of 1st 5-minute candle of open session
- **Open Strategy #4** - mark high and low of 1st 15-minute candle of open session
- **Oscillators** - indicators identifying overbought/oversold conditions
- **PDT Rule** - Pattern Day Trader rule restricting frequent trades
- **Price Action** - movement of a security's price over time
- **Profit/Pivot Level** - key level indicating potential price reversals
- **Relative Strength Index (RSI)** - momentum indicator measuring price changes
- **Resistance Levels** - price level where selling pressure is anticipated
- **Scalping** - quick trades for small profits
- **Scalping Indicator** - volume tool that includes percentage of buyers vs sellers
- **Scanners** - tools for scanning the market with trader's chosen search criteria

- **Simple Moving Average (SMA) -** average price over a specific period
- **Standard Volume -** normal trading volume tool for a chart
- **Support & Resistance -** key levels where price often reverses
- **Time & Sales (T&S) -** real-time data on executed trades
- **Trade Order Tool -** software for placing and managing trades
- **Trading Fees -** costs associated with executing trades
- **Trading Long -** buying securities expecting price increases
- **Trading Short -** selling borrowed securities expecting price decreases
- **Volume Weighted Average Price (VWAP) -** average price of a stock
- **Volatility Rating -** percentage rating reached by dividing the ATR revenue into the breakout range, where a rating of 25% or less indicates a better chance for a breakout at premarket levels when trading the Open Strategies
- **Volume Histogram -** graph showing volume of trades over time
- **Volume Profile (VP) -** chart showing volume traded at various price levels
- **Watchlists -** list of stocks being considered for potential trading

Notes & Reminders

Notes & Reminders

Notes & Reminders

Notes & Reminders

Made in the USA
Las Vegas, NV
12 October 2024

96713527R00103